BARBECUING THE weber® COVERED WAY

PUBLISHER: R. ARTHUR BARRETT
EDITORS: CAROL D. BRENT
AND
BETTY A. HUGHES
ART DIRECTOR: DICK COLLINS
PHOTOGRAPHY BY BILL MILLER

PUBLISHED FOR THE WEBER-STEPHEN
PRODUCTS COMPANY BY

trp®

TESTED RECIPE PUBLISHERS, INC. CHICAGO
A DIVISION OF JOHN BLAIR & COMPANY

contents

REVISED EDITION
Library of Congress Catalog Card Number 72-85084

Copyright © 1979 and 1972
by Tested Recipe Publishers, Inc.
Published in U.S.A. by Tested Recipe Publishers, Inc.
a Division of John Blair & Company, 6701 Oakton
Street, Chicago, Illinois 60648. Printed in U.S.A. by
American Printers and Lithographers, Inc., Chicago,
Illinois 60648.

introduction

Weber Kettle Cooking opens a whole new world of food enjoyment to both novice and expert cooks. Whether your purchase was a Weber Charcoal or Gas Covered Kettle, you will enjoy preparing the traditional barbecue foods as well as the great number of specialties possible only with a Weber Covered Kettle.

Kettle fans use their covered grills for complete outdoor meals and as a supplement to kitchen range and oven. You can broil, bake, roast, braise, stew, barbecue and grill. Appetizers, soups, stews, chops, vegetables, roasts, desserts, even hot beverages are easy to fix in a Weber Kettle.

The Weber cover reflects heat for even cooking. The cover also shortens cooking times and uses fuel more efficiently than any other barbecue method. Cooking covered frees the chef, too. You don't need to watch covered foods as closely as foods barbecued by another method.

Weber Covered Kettles are simple to use. Read the directions on the next pages for specific instructions for Charcoal or Gas, follow the recipes and that new world of cooking is yours!

ISBN 0-88351-002-2
SEVENTH PRINTING

COOKING IS EASY WITH A WEBER KETTLE

Outdoor cooking is almost effortless for the chef who has a Weber Kettle.

Heat is reflected off the Weber Kettle cover and the food cooks evenly on all sides without loss of juices and flavors. This even cooking means you dont *have to watch the food or the fire as closely as with other units.*

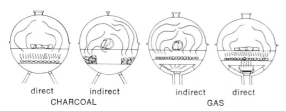

direct   indirect   indirect   direct
CHARCOAL   **GAS**

CHARCOAL BARBECUING
GENERAL INSTRUCTIONS

Open all dampers on bottom of kettle and on the cover. Remove cover and hang it on side of kettle with hook located inside cover, until coals are ready for cooking. Remove cooking (upper) grill. Arrange briquettes on charcoal (lower) grill for direct or indirect method of cooking. Ignite briquettes with charcoal lighter fluid or an electric fire starter. Let briquettes burn until they are covered with a light layer of gray ash. It is important to follow the instructions that come with the particular fire starter you use. Solid and semisolid starters are also safe to use. Follow the directions on the package.

NOTE: DO NOT USE GASOLINE, ALCOHOL OR OTHER HIGHLY FLAMMABLE FLUIDS TO IGNITE BRIQUETTES. NEVER ADD STARTER FLUID TO HOT OR EVEN WARM COALS.

Any excess fluid in the bottom of the kettle should be evaporated or burned off before you start to cook. When a drip pan is used, it is best to position it after fire has been arranged and you are ready to start cooking.

It usually takes 25 to 30 minutes for the fire to be ready for cooking. If fire gets too hot, it can be regulated by adjusting the dampers in the bottom of the kettle. Partially close dampers to reduce heat, leave them wide open for highest heat. The top damper should always remain open while cooking. Keep kettle covered when cooking except where otherwise directed.

When finished cooking, close all dampers and fire will go out.

DIRECT METHOD

This method of cooking is used primarily for fast cooking of flat meats (steaks, hamburgers, hot dogs, etc.) generally meats that requre less than 30 minutes cooking time. The Direct Method is the same for all size Weber Charcoal Kettles.

Here's how it's done:

1. Cover surface of charcoal (lower) grill with briquettes, one layer deep.
2. Heap these briquettes in center of charcoal grill and ignite.
3. When coals have formed a gray ash, spread burning coals over charcoal grill. Put cooking (upper) grill in place.

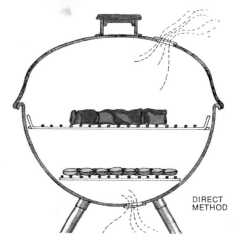

DIRECT METHOD

4. Meat is placed on the cooking grill directly above the hot coals and must be turned to expose both sides to the heat. Follow timing for each side as indicated in the recipe for the particular type of meat.
5. When cooking is finished, close all dampers and the fire will go out.
6. IMPORTANT! Use lean meats; trim off any excess fat to prevent flare-ups.

INDIRECT METHOD

With the Weber Kettle this is the most commonly used method of barbecuing. This method will cook small, large, even great big roasts so they have a fine appearance, flavor and juiciness without the use of a rotisserie. This method of cooking is great for baking favorite breads, pies, cakes, casseroles, etc.

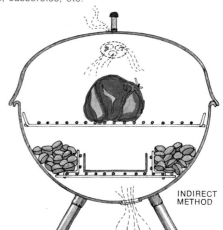

INDIRECT METHOD

Here's how it's done:

1. Position leg without a wheel (or place two bottom vents) into the wind and damper on cover away from the wind.
2. Arrange an equal number of charcoal briquettes on each side of the charcoal (lower) grill, on the sides of the kettle which do not have the outside handles. The use of charcoal rails will be helpful to keep charcoal in place and allow plenty of space in the center of grill for the aluminum foil drip pan. For number of briquettes to use, see chart on page 5.
3. Ignite briquettes and heat until covered with gray ash before starting to cook.
4. Make certain the coals are burning equally as well on both sides of the grill before beginning to cook. It

may be necessary to move hot coals from one side to the other in order to have the heat evenly distributed. Always use long handled tongs!

5. Place a heavy duty aluminum foil drip pan in center of charcoal grill. Drip pan should be in line with the outside kettle handles.
   If gravy is desired, center drip pan on cooking grill instead of charcoal grill. Use a roast holder to hold the meat out of the juices—place meat in the roast holder—then place roast holder with meat, inside the drip pan.
6. Position cooking grill with handles over coals so briquettes may be added as needed.
7. Cover kettle unless directed otherwise.
8. When cooking is finished, close all dampers and fire will go out.
9. Use barbecue mits when changing vents, removing cover, hot grill, foods, etc. or when moving grill.

How Many Briquettes to Use?

Barbecue Series	Size in inches	Briquettes needed on each side for first 45-50 min.	Number briquettes to add to each side every 45-50 min.
80000	26¾ Dia.	30	9
70000	22½ Dia.	25	8
30000	18½ Dia.	16	5
Smokey Joe	14¼ Dia.	9	4
Table Top	15½ x 9½	8	4

GAS BARBECUING

HOW TO LIGHT

1. Cover must be removed before lighting kettle. Hang cover on side of kettle with hook provided. Place Burner Control Knob in INDIRECT position.
2. Push Heat Control Knob in; turn to HIGH HEAT position.
3. Strike a long wooden kitchen or fireplace match; insert flaming tip into match hole.

DIRECT METHOD

This method is used primarily for searing or browning meats. Check and follow recipe directions for METHOD and HEAT to be used after searing or browning.

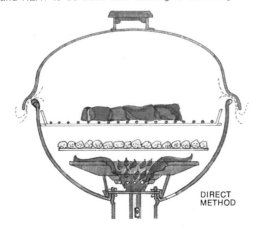

DIRECT METHOD

Preheat at DIRECT METHOD HIGH HEAT with cover on for 10 minutes.
When broiling meats they should be moved from one area of the grill to another as they are turned. This will help reduce flare-ups.

INDIRECT METHOD

This method (possible because of the unique design of the Weber Gas Kettle) is used for cooking most foods. It reduces the chance of flare-ups caused by direct flame.

There are 2 ways to use the INDIRECT METHOD:

INDIRECT METHOD HIGH HEAT—This method is used for flat meats (steaks, burgers, chops, etc.). Place lava rock over entire bottom grill. Drippings will then fall onto hot rocks, burn off and give zesty outdoor flavor to food being cooked.

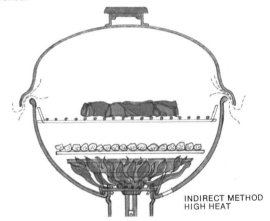

INDIRECT METHOD HIGH HEAT

Preheat kettle, *covered* at DIRECT METHOD HIGH HEAT for 10 minutes. Then place burner control in INDIRECT METHOD position. Food will cook by radiant heat.

INDIRECT METHOD LOW HEAT—This method is used for large, whole pieces of meat and for well-done meats. Remove cooking grill. Place lava rock over entire bottom of grill. Top rock in center with aluminum foil drip pan (page 6) slightly larger than piece of meat to be cooked. Replace cooking grill. Be sure that sides of drip pan are not bent down when replacing cooking grill. Position meat on cooking grill directly above drip pan. Pan must catch drippings to eliminate smoke.

Preheat kettle, *covered*, at INDIRECT METHOD HIGH HEAT for 10 minutes. Then switch to INDIRECT METHOD LOW HEAT before beginning to cook. Burner control must always be in INDIRECT position when using drip pan.

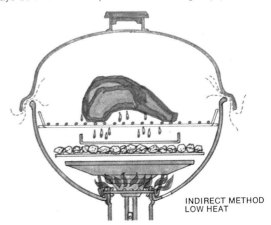

INDIRECT METHOD LOW HEAT

Make Your Own Aluminum Foil Pan For Indirect Cooking

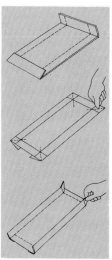

Use 18-inch heavy duty aluminum foil. Tear off a sheet which after being doubled will extend at least 3 inches beyond each end of meat being prepared. Fold, making a double thickness. Fold all edges over about 1½ to 2 inches.

Entire piece should now be flat. Turn piece over and use any sharp object or your fingernail and score all the way around 1 inch from edge. At corners score from point where scores cross, out to the corners.

Fold all edges up and pull out and pinch the corners. Fold corners back flat against sides.

WEBER KETTLES ARE EASY TO KEEP CLEAN

IN A HURRY? TRY THIS WAY:

CHARCOAL UNITS—Cover kettle; close dampers and cool kettle thoroughly.

GAS UNITS—Cover kettle. Turn gas off; cool kettle thoroughly.

BOTH UNITS—When kettle is cool, wipe outside and inside surfaces with damp cloth. NEVER use hose or water on kettle while hot! You can wait to clean the cooking grill until just before using the next time. Protect during storage by covering with Weber Vinyl Cover.

WHEN A GOOD CLEANING IS NEEDED, DO THIS:

CHARCOAL UNITS

1. Remove grills, charcoal and ashes.
2. Wash inside and outside of kettle and cover in warm water with a little detergent. Rinse and dry. When surface is badly coated with burned-on grease, use a good spray-type oven cleaner and follow directions on label. Rinse and dry.
3. Clean cooking grill with wire brush or a ball of crumpled aluminum foil. Wipe off any remaining residue with paper toweling.
4. Return grills to kettle; cover.
5. Protect during storage with Weber Vinyl Cover.

GAS UNITS

1. Remove grills and lava rocks.
2. Unscrew burner control knob; remove target burner and baffle.

3. Cover gas orifice with small piece of aluminum foil or plastic film, holding it in place with a rubber band.
4. Wash burner and baffle in warm water with a little mild detergent.
5. Proceed as directed in #2 and #3 under Charcoal Units at left.
6. Replace target burner, baffle, burner control knob, lava rocks and grills.
7. Protect during storage with Weber Vinyl Cover.

LAVA ROCKS are self cleaning. After cooking by DIRECT METHOD turn on HIGH for a few minutes and grease will burn off. If more cleaning is needed rocks may be boiled in water with a small amount of detergent. If cooking has been by HIGH HEAT DIRECT METHOD no burning off will be needed.

IMPORTANT DO'S AND DON'TS

Searing and browning are done with cover off. Cover can be hung on side of kettle when not in use. Hook is located inside cover.

Most cooking is done with cover on. Cover kettle unless directed otherwise. Of course you remove the cover to turn or baste foods.

Cover should always be left off the kettle while starting the fire.

COOKING TIMES AND TEMPERATURE OF FOODS

The cooking times suggested in this book are to be used as a guide only.

The recipes were developed for an outdoor temperature of 70°F. with little or no wind. If cooking is done on a cold and/or windy day cooking time will have to be increased.

Take meats directly from refrigerator to grill.

WEBER TIPS

BOTH UNITS—Occasionally wipe the inside of the cover with paper towels while it is still warm. It only takes a few minutes and will keep the grease from building up.

The cooking grill is best left uncleaned after cooking. The next time you barbecue, use a wire brush to remove all excess residue.

CHARCOAL GRILL—After approximately 8 hours of cooking, it is advisable to remove the accumulation of ashes. This is easily done by removing the cooking grill and the charcoal grill. Open the three bottom vents on the kettle and with some paper toweling, brush the ashes through the vent holes. Ashes will fall through to the ash catcher which can then be emptied.

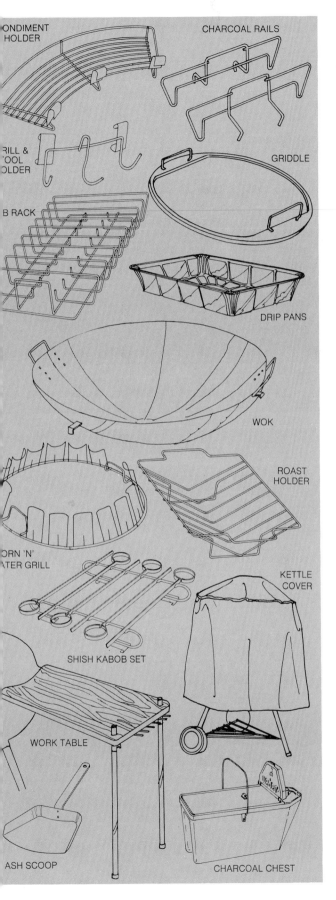

CONDIMENT HOLDER

CHARCOAL RAILS

GRILL & TOOL HOLDER

GRIDDLE

RIB RACK

DRIP PANS

WOK

ROAST HOLDER

CORN 'N' TATER GRILL

SHISH KABOB SET

KETTLE COVER

WORK TABLE

ASH SCOOP

CHARCOAL CHEST

WEBER ACCESSORIES TO MAKE COVERED COOKING EASIER

CONDIMENT HOLDER: Keeps salt, pepper, basting sauce, brush and whatever you need right at hand.

CHARCOAL RAILS: Make it easier to handle charcoal when cooking by INDIRECT METHOD. Rails slip over bottom grill and keep coals along sides of kettle away from drip pan. You can use rails with or without drip pan.

GRILL & TOOL HOLDER: Holds grill and tools right at the cooking area.

GRIDDLE: Great for breakfast or brunch. Pancakes, bacon, sausage and eggs cook beautifully. Japanese griddle cooking and stir-frying are great.

RIB RACK: Sturdy nickel plated rack, increases cooking capacity 50%. Can be used for chicken pieces, pork chops and ribs (see photo page 20). Eliminates double stacking and simplifies basting.

DRIP PANS: Heavy-gauge aluminum designed to drop into position for indirect cooking in any Weber Kettle.

WOK: Traditional steel pan for preparing Oriental foods outdoors. Open up a new world of cooking. Large capacity is great for a crowd.

CORN 'N' TATER GRILL: Nickel plated cooking ring (fits all 22-1/2'' Weber Kettles) prepares any combination of corn or potatoes to perfection. Allows space on cooking grill to cook meat with vegetables.

ROAST HOLDER: Great for roasting beef, lamb, pork, ham and poultry. The handles make it easy to transfer a heavy roast from grill to carving area.

SHISH KABOB SET: Sturdy Nickel-plated rack snaps on to cooking grill. Six heavy duty stainless steel skewers lock into rack.

KETTLE COVER: Heavy-duty vinyl protects grill and keeps it clean.

WORK TABLE: Beautiful Teak Veneer with utensil rack and adjustable aluminum legs. Fits 18-1/2'', 22-1/2'', 26-3/4'' charcoal and all Gas Grills.

ASH SCOOP: Makes ash disposal cleaner and easier. Contoured to fit the kettle.

CHARCOAL CHEST™: Sturdy weatherproof, heavy-duty with easy-pour spout. Keeps briquettes dry and handy! Fits on bottom shelf of kettle.

beef

MENU

Raw Vegetable Relishes and Chips
Favorite Assorted Cheese or Sour Cream Dips

CHARCOAL BROILED STEAK
Page 15
Bearnaise Sauce, *Page 60*
Potatoes Baked On Grill, *Page 67,* with Sour Cream
Corn In Husks, *Page 68*
Baked Tomato Halves, *Page 68*

TOSSED VEGETABLE SALAD
OR
PINEAPPLE CREAM SALAD
Page 64
Hot Dinner Rolls, *Page 56,* with Herb or
Apricot Butter, *Page 62*

Red Wine (Optional)

BAKED BANANAS
WITH ICE CREAM
Page 71
Coffee   Tea
Lemonade Coolers, *Page 75*

STANDING RIB ROAST

*A Favorite for Father's Day or
Special Occasion Dinners*

MENU

PICKLED SHRIMP
Assorted Fancy Crackers
Favorite Fruit, Tomato Juice or Clam Juice Cocktail

STANDING RIB ROAST
Page 11
Potatoes Baked On Grill, *Page 67*
Broccoli, *Page 67*
Barbecue Sauce, *Page 60*
Herb Butter, *Page 62*
Hollandaise Sauce, *Page 61*

Red Wine (Optional)

CAESAR SALAD
Page 65
(Assemble foods and equipment on cart and
let the host toss the salad)
Hot French or Italian Bread In Foil, *Page 56*
Garlic or Onion Butter, *Page 62*

STRAWBERRY GLAZED
CHEESE CAKE
Page 72
Coffee   Tea
Lemonade Coolers, *Page 75*

BEEF ROASTS

A perfectly roasted cut of beef is very special food, everyone's favorite meat. It requires little skill or attention to prepare and serve. Even a beginning cook can easily turn a fine cut of beef into a handsome and satisfying roast. Following a few simple directions will assure success.

TENDER CUTS

STANDING RIB ROAST
Excellent for serving a crowd, easy to prepare and serve. Part of rib section of the loin containing rib and back bone. Well-marbled lean meat, covered with a layer of white fat. Available in 3 to 7-rib roasts. Have meat man cut off short ribs and chine bone, loosen feather bones, remove back strap and tie securely for easy handling and carving. Prepackaged meats usually have short ribs, chine bone, etc. removed.

ROLLED RIB ROAST
Boneless. Same cut as standing rib roast except bones are removed and meat is rolled and tied (your meat man will do it). Wonderful for entertaining; easy to prepare and serve. Little waste.

RIB EYE, SPENCER OR DELMONICO ROAST
Boneless center or eye of rib roast. Have meat man tie securely to simplify handling and carving.

SIRLOIN TIP
Boneless, also called top sirloin roast or butt. Often rolled, covered with fat and tied securely. Little waste; easy to cook and serve.

TENDERLOIN
Boneless and very lean; the most expensive cut. Little waste, easy to roast and serve.

SHORT RIBS
Trimmed from end of standing rib roast. Short ribs vary in size. May be cut 1 to 2-ribs wide and 3 to 4-inches long. Large bone area covered with a small amount of meat and large amount of fat.

LESS TENDER CUTS

CHUCK OR ROUND
Blade or round bone. Purchase U.S. Choice or Prime grade beef and cut 1½ to 3-inches thick. Tenderize meat, if desired, with a commercial tenderizer or marinade, following label directions. To serve, slice thin on the diagonal.

EYE OF ROUND
Boneless, often covered with fat and tied securely. Tenderize, if desired, with a commercial tenderizer or marinade. To serve, slice thin on the diagonal.

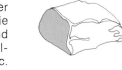

ROLLED RUMP ROAST
Boneless. Use U.S. Choice or Prime grade. Have meat man roll and tie securely. If roast has no fat covering, cover with foil while cooking or brush often with oil or basting sauce during roasting to keep surface moist.

How Much Beef To Buy?

Cooking and eating outdoors sharpens appetites and calls for generous servings. Select a large roast. Bigger roasts cook best and there's less waste. What's left can make tempting entrées and sandwiches for delicious hurry-up meals.

Cut	Serving allowance per person (raw weight)
Bone-in roasts	½ to 1 pound
Boneless roasts	⅓ to ½ pound
Short Ribs	¾ to 1¼ pounds

How To Cook Tender Beef Roasts

(Standing Rib, Rolled Rib, Rib Eye, Sirloin Tip, Tenderloin)

CHARCOAL—INDIRECT METHOD
GAS—INDIRECT METHOD LOW HEAT

Have meat man trim excess fat from roast and tie securely. Rub salt and pepper into meat. Insert meat thermometer into thickest part of roast with point away from bone and fat. Center roast, fat side up, in roast holder. Place on cooking grill directly over drip pan. If roast holder is not available stand roast, fat side up, on cooking grill over drip pan. Cover kettle; cook to the desired degree of doneness. A 10-pound roast takes about 15 to 20 minutes per pound to cook to 160°F. (medium).

Temperature Guide

Degree of Doneness	Cook to Internal Temperature of
Rare	140°F.
Medium	160°F.
Well-Done	170°F.

How To Cook Less Tender Beef Cuts

(Chuck, Round, Rump, etc.)

CHARCOAL—INDIRECT METHOD
GAS—INDIRECT METHOD LOW HEAT

Season meat as desired with salt and pepper. Place on cooking grill over drip pan. Cover kettle; roast to desired degree of doneness. An 8-pound rolled roast requires about 15 to 20 minutes per pound to cook to 160°F. (medium), more minutes per pound for smaller roast, fewer minutes per pound for larger roasts.

ARRANGEMENT OF ROAST IN WEBER KETTLES

CHARCOAL

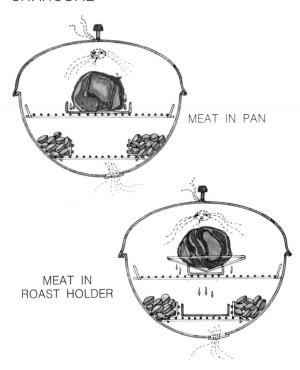

MEAT IN PAN

MEAT IN ROAST HOLDER

GAS

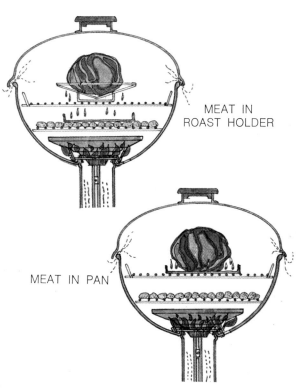

MEAT IN ROAST HOLDER

MEAT IN PAN

ROASTED BEEF TENDERLOIN

CHARCOAL—INDIRECT METHOD
GAS—INDIRECT METHOD LOW HEAT

Select whole or half (3 to 6-pound) beef tenderloin. Have meat man trim excess fat and tie meat securely every 1½ to 2 inches. Center meat on well-greased cooking grill directly over drip pan; cover kettle and cook to desired degree of doneness.

Tenderloin Timetable

Weight (Pounds)	Degree of Doneness	Cook to Internal Temperature	Approximate Cooking Time Minutes Per Pound
4 to 6	Rare	140°F.	12 to 15
	Medium	160°F.	15 to 18

Note: Cooking beef tenderloin to the well-done stage is not recommended.

ROLLED RUMP ROAST

CHARCOAL—INDIRECT METHOD
GAS—INDIRECT METHOD LOW HEAT

6 to 8-pound rolled beef rump roast
1½ teaspoons salt
¼ teaspoon pepper
Salad oil or a butter basting sauce (page 62)

Select U. S. Choice, Prime or Good grade roast. Rub salt and pepper into meat. Insert meat thermometer into center of thickest part of roast with point away from fat. Place in roast holder on cooking grill over drip pan. Cover kettle; cook about 2 hours to 160°F. (medium), or until meat is done. An 8-pound rolled rump roast requires 15 minutes per pound to reach 160°F. (medium). Yield: About 12 servings.

MEAT LOAF

CHARCOAL—INDIRECT METHOD
GAS—INDIRECT METHOD LOW HEAT

2 pounds ground chuck
½ cup chopped onion
¼ cup catsup
1 teaspoon prepared mustard
1 teaspoon salt
¼ teaspoon pepper
½ cup fine dry bread or corn flake crumbs
2 eggs
¼ cup milk
Salad oil
3 slices bacon, cut in half crosswise

Combine all ingredients except oil and bacon in a large bowl; mix well. Press meat mixture into a well-greased 9 x 5 x 3-inch loaf pan, smooth off top and brush with oil. Center pan on cooking grill; cover kettle and bake 30 minutes. Remove from grill; arrange bacon slices crosswise on top. Return to grill; cover and cook 30 to 40 minutes or until done. Yield: About 6 to 8 servings.

SAVORY POT ROAST

CHARCOAL—INDIRECT METHOD
GAS—INDIRECT METHOD LOW HEAT

4 pounds beef chuck (blade or round bone)
¼ cup wine or cider vinegar
¼ cup salad oil
¼ cup catsup
2 tablespoons soy sauce
2 tablespoons Worcestershire sauce
½ teaspoon rosemary
½ teaspoon garlic powder
½ teaspoon dry mustard

Brown meat on both sides on cooking grill over coals at sides of charcoal kettle, or in gas kettle with cover off using DIRECT METHOD HIGH HEAT. Turn meat with tongs. Switch gas kettle to INDIRECT METHOD LOW HEAT. Center meat on double thick square of heavy duty aluminum foil large enough to wrap around meat. Lift edges of foil slightly. Mix remaining ingredients; pour over roast. Seal foil edges tightly. Center roast on cooking grill. Cover kettle and cook 1 to 1½ hours, or until meat is fork tender. Transfer meat to heated platter; spoon sauce over meat. Yield: 4 to 6 servings.

BARBECUED SHORT RIBS

CHARCOAL—INDIRECT METHOD
GAS—INDIRECT METHOD LOW HEAT

4 to 5 pounds Choice grade beef short ribs
1 teaspoon salt
¼ teaspoon pepper
Weber's Tangy Barbecue Sauce (page 60)

Trim excess fat from ribs; season with salt and pepper. Brown ribs on cooking grill over coals at sides of charcoal kettle or in gas kettle with cover off using DIRECT METHOD HIGH HEAT. Turn meat with tongs. Switch gas kettle to INDIRECT METHOD LOW HEAT. Center ribs on cooking grill over drip pan; cover kettle and cook 1¼ to 1½ hours, or until meat is fork tender. Cooking time for less tender grades of meat will have to be increased to 1½ or 2 hours. Brush ribs with sauce 2 or 3 times during last 20 minutes of cooking. Yield: About 4 to 6 servings.

Know The Retail Steak Cuts

Confused about steak cuts in the retail stores? It is wise to be able to recognize commercial cuts and know how to cook them.

Steaks are available with bone-in or boneless in a tremendous variety of shapes, sizes, grades and prices. But, there's a delicious steak priced right for every budget.

Select beef that is firm, fine-grained and a bright cherry-red color. It should be marbled with thin streaks of fat and covered with a layer of flaky fat on outside edge.

Buy the best grade of steak possible, U.S. Prime, Choice or Good or quality branded steaks. If price is too high for top grade tender steaks buy top grade less tender steaks.

Less Tender Less Expensive Steaks

CHUCK
An economical steak with fine flavor. Select a top grade blade or 7-bone steak. Excellent for broiling, usually without tenderizing. Round bone steaks are usually tenderized with a marinade or commercial meat tenderizer. A delicious and inexpensive steak to serve a crowd.

ROUND
Top, bottom or full round steaks are also ideal for serving a crowd inexpensively. Tenderize with marinade or commercial meat tenderizer if desired.

Standing Rib Roast page 11

FLANK
Top grade flank steak is used for London Broil. Flank steak broils quickly to the rare stage. Slice diagonally very thin across the grain. Inexpensive, but fine eating.

Tender More Expensive Steak Cuts

PORTERHOUSE or LARGE T-BONE
One of the finest steak cuts from the large end of the short loin. Has a T-shaped bone and contains a generous section of the tenderloin. Steak serves several if 1½ to 2-inches thick. Very tender; one of the more expensive cuts.

T-BONE
Similar to the Porterhouse steak except it is smaller in size and has a smaller section of tenderloin. Usually a single serving cut.

STRIP
Boneless or bone-in. A tender cut from the top loin. Often called a Kansas City steak or New York cut. Usually a single serving cut.

RIB
Cut from the first 3 ribs. Modestly priced, comes boneless or bone-in. Usually a single serving.

SIRLOIN
Pin, flat or wedge-boned steaks are cut from the loin. Probably the most popular steak for broiling on the grill. A tender steak that serves several.

RIB EYE
The eye of the rib, sometimes called a Delmonico or Spencer steak. Very lean, deliciously tender, usually a single serving steak.

CLUB
Cut from the small end of the loin. A tender single serving steak.

FILET MIGNON AND CHATEAUBRIAND
A thick cut from the tenderloin. Center cuts are used for chateaubriand, the ends for filet mignon. Both are very tender. The most expensive steak cuts.

Steak Cooking Chart—Charcoal Or Gas Kettles

Thickness of Steak	Rare		Medium		Well Done	
	1st side	2nd side	1st side	2nd side	1st side	2nd side
1 inch	3 min.	3-4 min.	4 min.	4-5 min.	5 min.	6 min.
1½ inches	5 min.	6 min.	7 min.	8 min.	9 min.	10-11 min.
2 inches	7 min.	8 min.	9 min.	9-10 min.	10 min.	11-12 min.

STEAK BROILED IN GAS KETTLE

GAS—INDIRECT METHOD HIGH HEAT

Porterhouse, T-bone, Club, Sirloin or Tenderloin
Steak, 1 to 2-inches thick
Melted butter, margarine, salad oil or a butter
basting sauce (page 62)
Salt, as desired (½ to 1 teaspoon per pound
of meat)
Pepper, as desired

Trim excess fat from outer edges. Slash fat left on edge of steak at 1½ to 2 inch intervals to prevent curling during cooking. Center steak on cooking grill. Sear 1 minute on each side with cover off using DIRECT METHOD HIGH HEAT. When second side is seared, move steak to outer area of grill. Switch to INDIRECT METHOD HIGH HEAT. Place cover on kettle and cook on 1st side. (See cooking chart for approximate time). Turn steak with tongs or spatula, moving the meat back into center area of cooking grill. Cover and cook to desired degree of doneness. Remove steak from the grill and season with salt and pepper.

CHARCOAL BROILED STEAK

CHARCOAL—DIRECT METHOD

Porterhouse, T-bone, Club, Sirloin or Tenderloin
Steak, 1 to 2-inches thick
Salt, as desired (½ to 1 teaspoon salt per pound
of meat)
Pepper, as desired

Slash fat at edge of steak at 1½ to 2 inch intervals to prevent curling during cooking. Place steak on cooking grill. Cover kettle and cook on first side (see cooking chart above for approximate time). Turn steak with tongs; cover and cook on second side to desired degree of doneness (see cooking chart above). Remove from grill; season with salt and pepper to taste and serve at once.

If you prefer searing the steak, leave the cover off for the first minute only on each side.

Chuck Steak page 15

CHUCK STEAK RARE

CHARCOAL—INDIRECT METHOD
GAS—INDIRECT METHOD LOW HEAT

¾ cup salad oil
¾ cup cider or wine vinegar
1 clove garlic, crushed
2 teaspoons salt
½ teaspoon each of pepper and basil
5 to 6-pound Prime or Choice grade blade-bone
chuck steak, cut 2½ to 3-inches thick
Salt and pepper as desired

Combine first 5 ingredients; mix well. Place steak in large shallow baking dish or plastic bag. Cover steak with oil-vinegar mixture. Cover or close bag tightly. Refrigerate 12 to 24 hours, turning steak several times. Drain steak, reserving marinade. Rub cooking grill with suet or brush with oil. Sprinkle top and bottom of steak with salt and pepper as desired. Insert meat thermometer into center of thickest part of steak with point away from bone or fat. Center steak on cooking grill. Cover kettle and cook about 1½ to 1¾ hours to 140°F. (rare). (This steak is for fanciers of rare beef.)

To check doneness of steak if meat thermometer is not available, make a small cut to center of steak and check the color. Brush steak with leftover marinade several times during last 45 minutes of cooking. Slice steak very thin and diagonally across the grain. Yield: 10 to 12 servings.

Dressed Suckling Pig—ready for roasting.

Here's the line-up for the cook-out event of the year!

MENU

Tray of Melon, Assorted Fruit and
Shrimp arranged on Lemon Leaves
Weber's Cocktail Sauce, *Page 61*
Celery Seed Salad Dressing*
Coconut Chips, Salted Macadamia Nuts and
Assorted Fancy Crackers*
Tropical Fruit Punch (Any Combination of Fruit
Juices with Strawberry or Vanda Orchid Garnish)

ROASTED PIG, ISLAND-STYLE
Page 22
OR
ROASTED PORK LOIN
Page 21
Poi*
Parsleyed Rice Garnished with Baked Bananas
Page 71
Sweet Potatoes Baked In 'Tater Grill, *Page 68*
Baked Tomato Halves, *Page 68*
Zucchini, *Page 67*

FRUIT SALAD IN MELON BOWL
Page 64
Assorted Relishes and Pickles*
Hot Rolls

ICE CREAM COCONUT BALLS**
with Pineapple or Fresh Strawberry Sauce
Fruit Drinks in Fresh Pineapple Shells
with Sherbet and Mint Sprigs · OR   Iced Tea

*Available in specialty food stores or gourmet
shops.
**Roll vanilla ice cream balls in flaked coconut.
Store in freezer until serving time.

To Serve . . .

The traditional feast of the Hawaiian Islands is called
a Luau. The setting for a luau should be one of lush
greenery, brilliant blossoms and tantalizing foods.

The luau may be served on the ground, island-style,
but if the guests are neither young nor limber spread
the banquet on a large table. Cover table or ground
with several layers of newspapers, then cover papers
with leaves and fishnet, a straw mat or an Hawaiian
cloth. Arrange an attractive setting with ferns and
greenery (plants or leaf sprays) and flowers. Build
a centerpiece of fruits and flowers and add torches
or candles, as desired.

Large wooden trays make attractive serving pieces.
Wooden or brightly-colored paper serving plates
help make the meal more festive.

Tropical Leaves Available . . .

Ti, lemon or gardenia leaves, palm fronds, ferns
and tropical plants are usually available at the flor-
ists. It is best to order them a few days in advance.

Flowers With A Feel Of The Islands . . .

Gardenias, Vanda or other orchids, hibiscus, leis of
all types, tropical flowers, carnations, anthuriums
and tuberus begonias are generally available, if ordered ahead of time.

Fruits . . .

Melons, fresh pineapples, papaya, mangoes, grapefruit, oranges, lemons, limes, grapes, berries, coco-
nuts, etc. are available at fine produce stores in
most cities.

PORK AND HAM
Always tempting cook-out favorites!

Sizzling pork and ham roasts, spareribs and chops are ever-popular for backyard barbecues.

Fresh pork and hams are better and leaner than ever. Breeders are raising leaner animals and any excess fat is trimmed off, leaving just enough to make the meat tender and juicy.

Selecting fine fresh pork is easy even though the cuts are not graded Prime, Choice, etc., as are beef and lamb. The lean is firm, fine-grained, has a gray-pink color and a uniform covering of fat to protect the lean.

Hams, picnics and Canadian bacon or smoked pork shoulder are available fully-cooked and need only to be heated and browned, others are uncooked and require a full cooking. Hams and smoked pork shoulders are available boneless or bone-in. Most cured and smoked meats are sold in their original casing and are labeled. Read the labels carefully, they will state the type of product and the cooking required before serving.

Favorite Pork Cuts For Barbecuing

LOINS
Bone-in center cut pork loin (4 to 6-pounds) is best. Loin ends roast equally well and are usually less expensive. Have meat man saw backbone from rib bones to make carving easier.

FRESH HAM
Bone-in or boneless, rolled and tied; same cut as ham except it is fresh pork and requires cooking to 170°F. (well-done).

PORK SHOULDER
Bone-in or boneless, rolled and tied, weighs 4 to 6-pounds. Must be fully cooked to 170°F.

CHOPS
Fresh or smoked. Must be fully cooked. For best results cut chops 1 to 2-inches thick.

SPARERIBS, BABY RIBS OR BACKRIBS
Come in slabs. Backribs are the most meaty. Baby ribs are small, ideal for snacks or appetizers. All ribs must be cooked to well-done stage.

HAMS WHOLE OR HALF
Bone-in and boneless rolled hams are available fully-cooked or cured and requiring full cooking. Hams weigh 10 to 14-pounds, even bigger if desired. The smaller hams usually are finer-grained, more juicy and tender.

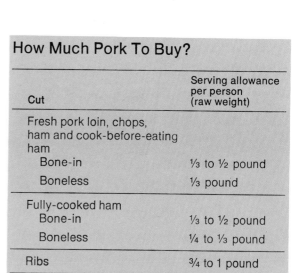

How Much Pork To Buy?

Cut	Serving allowance per person (raw weight)
Fresh pork loin, chops, ham and cook-before-eating ham	
Bone-in	⅓ to ½ pound
Boneless	⅓ pound
Fully-cooked ham	
Bone-in	⅓ to ½ pound
Boneless	¼ to ⅓ pound
Ribs	¾ to 1 pound

PORK CHOP CASSEROLE

CHARCOAL—INDIRECT METHOD
GAS—INDIRECT METHOD LOW HEAT

6 pork chops, 1-inch thick
2 tablespoons butter or margarine
6 slices (¼-inch) Spanish onion
1 cup uncooked rice
1 can (1 pound) stewed tomatoes
1 can (10½ ounces) condensed chicken broth
1¼ cups water
1 teaspoon salt
1 teaspoon oregano
½ teaspoon thyme
½ teaspoon minced parsley
Dash of pepper

Brown chops in butter or margarine; arrange in a 9 x 13 x 2-inch baking pan or dish. Top each chop with an onion slice. Pour rice around chops. Distribute tomatoes, broth, water and seasonings evenly over chops. Cover tightly with aluminum foil; center on cooking grill. Cover kettle and cook about 1 hour, or until chops are fork tender. Yield: 6 servings.

GRILLED OR BARBECUED PORK CHOPS

(Loin, Shoulder or Rib Chops)

CHARCOAL—INDIRECT METHOD
GAS—INDIRECT METHOD LOW HEAT

Trim any excess fat from chops. Brown fresh or smoked loin, rib or shoulder chops (cut 1 to 2-inches thick) on cooking grill over coals at sides of charcoal kettle, or in gas kettle with cover off using DIRECT METHOD HIGH HEAT. Turn chops with tongs as needed to brown evenly on both sides. Switch gas kettle to INDIRECT METHOD LOW HEAT. Transfer chops to center of cooking grill directly over drip pan or arrange chops in rib rack over drip pan. Cover kettle and cook until meat is well-done (see suggested time below). Brush chops often with butter basting sauce (page 62) during last 15 minutes. If desired, a barbecue sauce (pages 60 and 61) may be subsituted for basting sauce during last 15 minutes of cooking.

Pork Chop Cooking Chart— Charcoal Or Gas Kettle

Thickness of Chops	Approximate Cooking Time (minutes)	
	First Side	Second Side
1-inch	15 to 18	15 to 18
1½-inch	20 to 25	18 to 20
2-inches	28 to 30	26 to 30

All pork chops must be cooked to well-done (170°F. internal temperature)

SWEET-SOUR PORK CHOPS

CHARCOAL—INDIRECT METHOD
GAS—INDIRECT METHOD LOW HEAT

6 butterfly pork chops, 1-inch thick
½ cup Sauterne or other white wine
½ cup pineapple juice
¼ cup lemon juice
¼ cup soy sauce
2 tablespoons honey
2 tablespoons Worcestershire sauce
1 tablespoon prepared mustard
1 teaspoon salt
½ teaspoon hot red pepper sauce
½ teaspoon onion powder
Dash of pepper
2 cups drained, canned or fresh pineapple chunks

Brown chops on cooking grill over coals at sides of charcoal kettle, or in gas kettle with cover off using DIRECT METHOD HIGH HEAT. Turn chops with tongs as needed to brown evenly. Switch gas kettle to INDIRECT METHOD LOW HEAT. Remove chops from grill; place in 9 x 13 x 2-inch or larger baking pan. Combine and mix all remaining ingredients except pineapple chunks. Pour over chops. Center pan on cooking grill; cover kettle. Cook 1 to 1¼ hours or until done, basting chops often. Add pineapple chunks last 15 minutes of cooking time. Yield: 6 servings.

BAKED PORK CHOPS

CHARCOAL—INDIRECT METHOD
GAS—INDIRECT METHOD LOW HEAT

Season chops with salt and pepper; center chops on cooking grill and brown with cover off using DIRECT METHOD HIGH HEAT. Turn chops with tongs as needed to brown evenly on both sides. Remove chops from grill; place in aluminum foil tray. Switch to INDIRECT METHOD LOW HEAT. Place tray on cooking grill. Cover kettle and cook about 55 minutes or until done.

SAUCY PORK CHOPS

CHARCOAL—INDIRECT METHOD
GAS—INDIRECT METHOD LOW HEAT

6 pork chops, ¾-inch thick
1 teaspoon salt
¼ teaspoon pepper
1 can (10½ ounces) cream of chicken soup
1 medium onion, sliced
3 tablespoons catsup
2 tablespoons Worcestershire sauce

Brown chops on cooking grill over coals at sides of charcoal kettle, or in gas kettle with cover off using DIRECT METHOD HIGH HEAT. Turn chops with tongs as needed to brown evenly. Sprinkle with salt and pepper. Switch gas kettle to INDIRECT METHOD LOW HEAT. Arrange chops in 9 x 13 x 2-inch baking pan or dish. Combine remaining ingredients; mix well. Pour sauce over chops. Cover tightly with aluminum foil; center on cooking grill. Cover kettle and cook 50 to 60 minutes or until chops are fork tender. Yield: 4 to 6 servings.

SMOKY COUNTRY BARBECUED RIBS

CHARCOAL—INDIRECT METHOD
GAS—INDIRECT METHOD LOW HEAT

6 pounds lean spareribs
2 or 3 tablespoons liquid smoke
2 teaspoons salt
1 cup catsup
1 cup water
½ cup firmly-packed brown sugar
¼ cup vinegar
2 tablespoons Worcestershire sauce
1 teaspoon chili powder
½ teaspoon celery seed
½ teaspoon pepper

Cut ribs into 4-rib sections; brush on both sides with liquid smoke; refrigerate 30 minutes. Arrange ribs in rib rack or shallow roasting pan; center on cooking grill. Sprinkle with salt. Cover kettle; cook about 1¾ to 2 hours, or until ribs are very tender and nicely browned. Combine and mix remaining ingredients. Brush over ribs several times during last 45 minutes of cooking. Serve ribs with remaining sauce. Yield: About 6 servings.

How Much Ham To Buy?

Ham	Approximate servings per pound
Boneless	
Fully-cooked	3 to 4
Cook-before-eating	2 to 3
Bone-in	
Fully-cooked	2 to 3
Cook-before-eating	2

SPARERIBS OR BACKRIBS

CHARCOAL—INDIRECT METHOD
GAS—INDIRECT METHOD LOW HEAT

6 pounds spareribs or backribs
1½ teaspoons salt
Weber's Tangy Barbecue Sauce (page 60)

Cut ribs in 4-rib sections; sprinkle with salt. Stand ribs upright in rib rack on cooking grill over drip pan. Cover kettle; cook 1 hour 20 minutes to 1 hour 30 minutes or until meat is tender and browned. Baste ribs 3 or 4 times with barbecue sauce the last 30 minutes of cooking. Yield: 6 servings.

Another Way To Barbecue Ribs...

Cut ribs and season as above. Brown ribs on cooking grill over coals at sides of charcoal kettle. Turn with tongs as needed to brown evenly. Arrange ribs in center of cooking grill. Proceed as above.

ROASTED PORK LOIN

CHARCOAL—INDIRECT METHOD
GAS—INDIRECT METHOD LOW HEAT

4 to 6-pound boneless or bone-in pork loin
2½ teaspoons salt
⅛ teaspoon pepper
Favorite basting sauce (page 62)

Sprinkle pork loin with salt and pepper. Insert meat thermometer in center of thickest part of roast with point away from bone and fat. Center meat on cooking grill over drip pan. Cover kettle and cook to 170°F. (well-done), about 17 minutes per pound for charcoal or 20 minutes per pound for gas. Brush roast with pan drippings or basting sauce 3 or 4 times during last 15 minutes of cooking. Let stand 10 to 15 minutes before serving. Yield: About 6 or 8 servings.

BAKED HAM

CHARCOAL—INDIRECT METHOD
GAS—INDIRECT METHOD LOW HEAT

Whole or half boneless or bone-in fully-cooked
(ready-to-eat), canned, or cured and smoked
(cook-before-eating) ham
Whole cloves
Brown Sugar Glaze (recipe follows)
Canned pineapple slices, well-drained
Maraschino cherries

Read directions before removing wrappings from ham. If necessary cut off rind. Score fat criss-cross fashion with sharp knife, making very shallow cuts so juices will not escape. Stud with whole cloves. Insert meat thermometer into center of thickest part of ham, with point away from bone and fat. Center ham, fat side up, on cooking grill directly above drip pan. Cover kettle. Cook cook-before-eating hams to 160°F., about 12 minutes per pound for an 8 to 10 pound ham or 16 minutes per pound for 16 pound ham. Fully-cooked and canned hams need only be heated to serving temperature, 140°F., about 9 minutes per pound in charcoal kettle or 13 minutes per pound in gas kettle. Baste ham with Brown Sugar Glaze during last 30 minutes of cooking. Garnish with pineapple slices and cherries 10 minutes before end of cooking time; brush with glaze and allow fruit to heat.

BROWN SUGAR GLAZE

Combine ½ cup firmly-packed brown sugar, 3 tablespoons water and 2 teaspoons prepared mustard in small saucepan; mix and heat until sugar melts. Brush over ham and fruit.

ROASTED PIG, ISLAND-STYLE

CHARCOAL—INDIRECT METHOD
GAS—INDIRECT METHOD LOW HEAT

12 to 15-pound oven-ready suckling pig
  (order from meat man several days in advance)
½ cup soy sauce
⅓ cup salad oil
¼ cup sherry
¼ cup firmly-packed brown sugar
1½ teaspoons salt
½ teaspoon pepper
1 clove garlic, crushed
Macadamia Nut Stuffing (recipe this page)
Ti or galax leaves, washed and dried
Limes and fresh in-season fruit for garnishing
Watercress or mint leaves

Wash pig under cold running water; pat dry, inside and outside, with paper towels. Combine and mix soy sauce, oil, sherry, sugar, salt, pepper and garlic. Let stand 20 to 30 minutes. Brush entire cavity of pig with marinade and save remaining marinade. Refrigerate pig until time to stuff and roast.

Before stuffing pig, again brush cavity with marinade. Fill loosely with Macadamia Nut Stuffing. Close cavity by skewering cavity opening and lacing skewers together with heavy white cord. Stuff a lime, cube of wood or hard ball of aluminum foil into pig's mouth to hold jaws open during roasting. Cover ears, tail, nose and front feet with small pieces of aluminum foil to prevent burning. Remove foil from tail, ears, nose and feet one hour before end of cooking time. Skewer back feet forward under pig. Place pig in kneeling position, front feet forward on well-greased cooking grill over heavy metal drip pan filled with 2 cups of water. Brush pig with reserved marinade. To keep skin from splitting prick skin with large needle several places behind head. Insert meat thermometer in thickest part of thigh with point away from bone and fat.

Cover kettle; cook until meat is tender. Baste frequently with reserved marinade or oil. Allow 25 minutes per pound to cook a 10 to 15-pound pig to 170°F. (well-done). Be sure meat is fully cooked! If there is a trace of pink in juices, continue roasting. Juices from well-done pig will have a light yellow color. Let pig stand 20 to 30 minutes before carving.

Arrange pig on large wooden platter or cutting board edged with ti or galax leaves. Remove brace from pig's mouth; replace with a fresh lime. Remove skewers and string. Push a small maraschino cherry in each eye and secure with wooden picks. Garnish platter and pig with an assortment of favorite in-season fresh fruits and watercress or mint. Yield: 8 to 10 servings.

MACADAMIA NUT STUFFING

4 cups ¼-inch cubes soft white bread, about
  8 slices
3 cups crumbled corn bread
½ cup coarsely chopped onion
½ cup finely diced celery
½ cup butter or margarine
1 cup well-drained canned crushed pineapple
½ cup chopped Macadamia nuts or pecans
2 eggs, beaten
1 teaspoon salt
¼ teaspoon pepper

Combine bread cubes and corn bread crumbs in large bowl. Cook onion and celery in butter or margarine until onion is tender. Add to bread mixture; toss lightly. Add remaining ingredients; toss until well mixed. Any excess stuffing may be spooned into pan, covered, and cooked along with pig during last 45 minutes of roasting. Yield: Enough dressing to fill a 15-pound pig.

Note: Pig should be cooked immediately after stuffing. Any stuffing that doesn't fit into pig must be refrigerated until cooking time. If any stuffing is left-over after pig is cooked and served, remove immediately after dinner and refrigerate separately.

BAKED PORK TENDERLOIN

CHARCOAL—INDIRECT METHOD
GAS—INDIRECT METHOD LOW HEAT

2 whole pork tenderloins (about 1 pound each)
½ cup butter or margarine
½ pound fresh mushrooms, cleaned and sliced
1 cup chopped celery
1 medium onion, sliced
1 chicken or vegetable bouillon cube
¾ cup water
2 tablespoons flour
2 teaspoons salt
¼ teaspoon pepper
¼ cup sherry

Lightly brown pork in butter or margarine in skillet. Place meat in shallow baking dish. Add mushrooms, celery and onion to skillet and cook until onion is tender, about 5 minutes. Crush bouillon cube in water and stir until dissolved. Stir into flour, salt and pepper; blend until smooth. Add to vegetables. Cook until thickened, stirring constantly. Stir in sherry. Pour sauce over meat; cover baking dish with foil and place on cooking grill. Cover kettle, cook about 1½ hours or until meat is tender. Slice meat and serve with sauce. Yield: 6 servings.

HAM STEAK WITH CHERRY GLAZE

CHARCOAL—INDIRECT METHOD
GAS—INDIRECT METHOD LOW HEAT

1 jar (12 ounces) cherry preserves
3 tablespoons orange or lemon juice
2 slices fully-cooked ham, 1-inch thick

Combine and mix preserves and orange or lemon juice; heat and set aside. Center ham slices on cooking grill directly over drip pan; cover kettle and cook 15 minutes. Turn and brush ham with cherry glaze. Cook about 15 minutes or until nicely browned. Serve with remaining sauce. Yield: About 6 servings.

CROWN ROAST OF PORK

CHARCOAL—INDIRECT METHOD
GAS—INDIRECT METHOD LOW HEAT

8 to 10-pound crown roast of pork
1½ to 2 teaspoons salt
Mushroom Stuffing (recipe this page)
3 tablespoons orange marmalade, melted

Season roast inside and outside with salt. Place roast on greased circle (the size of the roast) of double thick heavy duty aluminum foil. Fill center cavity with Mushroom Stuffing. Place roast on another double thick sheet of foil on cooking grill directly over drip pan. Cover top of stuffing with a circle of foil; pierce foil with tines of fork. Cover kettle. Cook about 25 to 35 minutes per pound or 3 to 3½ hours, depending upon size of roast. About 15 minutes before roast is done brush all meat surfaces with melted marmalade; remove foil from stuffing and allow to brown. Pork must be cooked to 170°F. (well-done). Yield: 10 to 12 servings.

MUSHROOM STUFFING

1 can (4 ounces) sliced mushrooms
⅓ cup butter or margarine
3 tablespoons minced onion
4 cups ¼-inch cubes bread, about 8 slices
⅓ cup finely chopped celery
1 teaspoon sage
1 teaspoon salt
⅛ teaspoon pepper

Drain mushrooms, reserving liquid. Melt butter or margarine in skillet with heatproof handle. Add onion; cook until tender. Combine remaining ingredients and mushrooms in large bowl; mix well. Add onion-butter mixture and mushroom liquid; mix well. Add water if additional liquid is needed.

Your Greek dinner starts with a Weber-roasted leg of lamb.

GALA GREEK DINNER

You can take a culinary tour of Greece without leaving your backyard

MENU

Lemon Soup (Avgolemono)   OR   Tiny Dolmas*

LEG OF LAMB, GREEK-STYLE
Page 27
Grape Garnish
Rice Pilaf, *Page 27*
Green Beans, *Page 67*   Minted Peas, *Page 67*

Dry Red Wine   OR   Retsina

GREEK SALAD
(Shredded lettuce, chopped celery, sliced cucumber, tomatoes, green pepper, onion, Greek olives, anchovies, Greek Feta cheese, vinegar and olive oil dressing and oregano)

Bread Sticks   OR   Dinner Rolls
Butter

BAKLAVA
or Other Greek Pastries*

Turkish Coffee

*Available in specialty food stores or gourmet shops.

LAMB SHANK DINNER

Fix this feast for a Saturday night get-together

MENU

Chilled Tomato Juice
Assorted Crackers

LAMB SHANKS
Page 29
OR
STUFFED LAMB CHOPS
Page 28
Herb or Onion Baked Potato Quarters, *Page 68*
Asparagus Hollandaise, *Page 66*

CRANBERRY ORANGE SALAD
Page 64

Hot Biscuits   OR   Marmalade Rolls, *Page 57*

BRANDY ICE
Page 72
OR
Strawberry Shortcake

Coffee   or   Tea

Lamb—There's Nothing Better!

Lamb is tender in age and tender to eat. The Greeks have a wonderful way of barbecuing lamb. With a Weber Charcoal or Gas Kettle it's easy to prepare many a barbecued lamb dish with true old-world flavor.

Select one of the favorite traditional lamb cuts, described below, or have the meat man guide you to some of the newer lamb cuts. Select U.S. Prime, Choice or Good grade meat.

STEAKS
A steak cut from a leg of lamb or lamb shoulder makes a marvelous meal. Have steaks cut 1¼ to 2-inches thick for finest flavor and juiciness.

ROASTS
The leg, shoulder and breast of lamb all make great roasts. Select bone-in or boneless.

RACK OF LAMB
The handsomest of lamb roasts. Select a 4 to 9-pound top grade rack for truly magnificent dining.

How Much Lamb To Buy?

Cut	Serving allowance per person (raw weight or pieces)
Chops	1 or 2 chops or ½ to ¾ pound
Steaks	½ to ¾ pound
Roasts	
Leg, Bone-in	½ to ¾ pound
Leg, Boneless	About ½ pound
Shoulder, Bone-in	½ to ¾ pound
Rack	½ to ¾ pound
	1 or 2 ribs

Favorite Lamb Cuts For Barbecuing

LAMB CHOPS
Center cut loin, rib or Frenched rib and shoulder chops. All are best cut 1½ to 2-inches thick. Center cut chops are considered the finest; rib and Frenched rib chops come in a close second. Shoulder chops, cut thick, are the best buy.

BONELESS LEG OF LAMB

CHARCOAL—INDIRECT METHOD
GAS—INDIRECT METHOD LOW HEAT

5 to 6-pound leg of lamb, boned, rolled and tied
2 cloves garlic, quartered
Olive or salad oil
1 tablespoon grated lemon peel
1½ teaspoons salt
1 teaspoon rosemary
¼ teaspoon black pepper

Using a small pointed knife make 8 small slits in surface of meat. Insert a sliver of garlic in each slit. Insert meat thermometer in center of thickest part of roast, with point away from fat. Brush meat with oil. Sprinkle lemon peel, salt, rosemary and pepper evenly over top. Center lamb on cooking grill directly over drip pan. Cover kettle; cook about 3 hours or until meat thermometer reaches 175°F. (medium). Yield: About 10 servings.

LAMBURGERS

CHARCOAL—DIRECT METHOD
GAS—INDIRECT METHOD HIGH HEAT

1 pound lean ground lamb
1 teaspoon salt
⅛ teaspoon pepper

Combine and mix lamb, salt and pepper; shape into 4 patties about ¾-inch thick. Arrange patties on cooking grill. Cook as directed for Steak Burgers (page 32). Yield: 4 patties.

LEG OF LAMB, GREEK-STYLE

CHARCOAL—INDIRECT METHOD
GAS—INDIRECT METHOD LOW HEAT

2 teaspoons salt
1½ teaspoons crushed oregano
½ teaspoon pepper
4 to 5-pound leg of lamb
1 cup water
1 can (8 ounces) tomato sauce
1 clove garlic, crushed
1 small lemon, thinly sliced
1 package (9 ounces) frozen artichoke hearts,
   separated

Combine salt, oregano and pepper; rub into lamb. Center lamb on cooking grill directly over drip pan. Cover kettle; cook 2½ hours. Remove lamb from kettle; place in uncovered roasting pan. Combine and mix remaining ingredients except lemon slices and artichokes; pour over lamb. Arrange lemon slices on lamb and surround with artichoke hearts. Return lamb in roasting pan to kettle, cover and cook about 45 to 60 minutes until meat is fork tender or meat thermometer reaches 175°F. (medium). Baste with sauce during last 45 minutes of cooking, if desired. Yield: About 10 servings.

RICE PILAF

CHARCOAL—INDIRECT METHOD
GAS—INDIRECT METHOD LOW HEAT

¼ cup butter, margarine or olive oil
⅓ cup finely chopped onion
½ clove garlic, crushed
½ cup hot water
1 chicken bouillon cube, mashed
6 cups hot cooked seasoned rice
1 can (4 ounces) mushroom pieces, drained
1½ tablespoons minced parsley
½ teaspoon oregano
¼ teaspoon basil, optional
⅓ cup toasted sliced almonds

On cooking grill heat butter, margarine or oil in large skillet with heatproof handle. Add onion, garlic, water and bouillon cube. Cook until onion is tender, but not brown. Stir in rice, mushroom pieces, parsley, oregano and basil; sprinkle with toasted almonds, cover with aluminum foil. Cover kettle and heat to serving temperature. Yield: 8 servings.

BARBECUED LAMB SPARERIBS

CHARCOAL—INDIRECT METHOD
GAS—INDIRECT METHOD LOW HEAT

4 pounds lamb spareribs
1½ teaspoons salt
Weber's Tangy Barbecue Sauce (page 60)

Trim excess fat from spareribs. Cut into 3 or 4-rib sections. Sprinkle with salt. Arrange in rib rack and center on cooking grill over drip pan. Cover kettle and cook about 1 hour and 10 to 20 minutes or until meat is tender and browned. Brush with sauce during last 20 minutes of cooking. Yield: 6 to 8 servings.

LAMB CHOPS

CHARCOAL—INDIRECT METHOD
GAS—INDIRECT METHOD LOW HEAT

6 to 8 lamb chops, 1 to 1½ -inches thick
1 to 1½ teaspoons salt
Pepper

Season chops with salt and pepper; brown chops on cooking grill over coals at sides of charcoal kettle or in gas kettle with cover off using DIRECT METHOD HIGH HEAT. Turn chops with tongs as needed to brown evenly. Switch gas kettle to INDIRECT METH-OD LOW HEAT. Remove cooking grill place drip pan in position. Replace cooking grill and arrange chops directly over drip pan. Cover kettle; cook about 20 to 25 minutes or until chops are tender. Yield: 3 to 4 servings.

SWEET AND SOUR LAMB CHOPS

CHARCOAL—INDIRECT METHOD
GAS—INDIRECT METHOD LOW HEAT

8 lamb shoulder chops, 1-inch thick
⅓ cup firmly-packed brown sugar
3 tablespoons wine vinegar
2 tablespoons lemon juice
½ cup water
1½ teaspoons salt
⅛ teaspoon pepper
8 small unpeeled orange slices, ¼-inch thick
2 tablespoons cornstarch
3 cups hot cooked seasoned rice

Brown chops on both sides on cooking grill over coals at sides of charcoal kettle or in gas kettle with cover off using DIRECT METHOD HIGH HEAT. Turn as needed with tongs to brown evenly. While chops are browning prepare sauce. Combine sugar, vinegar, lemon juice, ¼ cup water, salt and pepper. Mix well. Switch gas kettle to INDIRECT METHOD LOW HEAT. Arrange chops in shallow baking pan and pour sauce over meat. Top each chop with an orange slice. Place pan on cooking grill. Cover kettle; cook 25 to 30 minutes or until chops are tender. Spoon sauce over chops 2 or 3 times during cooking. Combine cornstarch and remaining ¼ cup water; mix. Transfer chops to heated serving platter. Stir cornstarch mixture into sauce and cook, stirring constantly, until smooth and thick. Pour sauce over chops. Serve with rice. Yield: 4 servings.

BARBECUED LAMB CHOPS

Follow recipe for Lamb Chops (page 27). Rub both sides of raw chops with cut garlic clove. Season and cook chops as directed for lamb chops, brushing with favorite commercial or homemade barbecue sauce (page 60).

LAMB STEAKS

Follow recipe for Lamb Chops (page 27), substituting 3 to 4 lamb steaks for the 6 to 8 lamb chops called for.

STUFFED LAMB CHOPS

CHARCOAL—INDIRECT METHOD
GAS—INDIRECT METHOD LOW HEAT

6 double lamb chops, 2-inches thick
½ cup flour
1½ teaspoons salt
¼ teaspoon pepper
2 cooking apples, cored and chopped
1 small onion, chopped
1 stalk celery, finely diced
1 cup well-drained cooked rice
½ cup well-drained crushed pineapple
¼ cup seedless raisins
1 teaspoon curry powder
½ teaspoon onion salt
½ teaspoon sugar

Cut a pocket in meaty side of chops. Combine an mix flour, salt and pepper. Coat chops with flou mixture. Combine and mix apples, onion and celery combine with all remaining ingredients. Mix well. Fi pockets in chops with stuffing. Wrap each chop in double thickness of heavy duty aluminum foil; sea edges securely. Wrap any extra stuffing in foil pack age and seal securely. Arrange on cooking grill Cover kettle and cook about 20 minutes; turn anc cook 25 to 30 minutes longer or until lamb is tender and fully cooked. Yield: 6 servings.

LAMB LOAF

CHARCOAL—INDIRECT METHOD
GAS—INDIRECT METHOD LOW HEAT

1½ pounds ground lean lamb
1½ cups soft bread crumbs
3 tablespoons minced onion
2 tablespoons finely chopped green pepper, optional
2 tablespoons bacon drippings, butter or
    margarine, melted
1 tablespoon minced parsley
1 teaspoon salt
1 teaspoon lemon juice
½ teaspoon garlic salt
1 egg
⅔ cup milk

Combine and mix all ingredients. Pack into well-greased 8½ x 4½ x 2½-inch loaf pan preferably aluminum foil; smooth off top. Center loaf pan on cooking grill; cover kettle and bake 1½ to 1¾ hours or until done. Let cool in pan 5 to 10 minutes before draining off juices and removing from pan. Yield: About 8 servings.

LAMB SHANKS

CHARCOAL—INDIRECT METHOD
GAS—INDIRECT METHOD LOW HEAT

6 lamb shanks
2 tablespoons salad oil
½ cup finely chopped celery
1 medium onion, thinly sliced
½ cup water
3 tablespoons lemon juice
1 teaspoon salt
⅛ teaspoon pepper
1 clove garlic, crushed
1 bay leaf
Pinch of basil

Brown shanks well in hot oil in skillet over moderate heat, turning shanks as needed to brown evenly. Transfer meat to 9 x 13 x 2-inch or other large metal pan. Mix remaining ingredients; pour over meat. Cover tightly with aluminum foil. Center pan on cooking grill; cover kettle and cook about 2 hours or until meat is fork tender. Yield: 6 servings.

burgers and sausage

The Weber Kettle Chef is a man for all seasons. He cooks outdoors summer, winter, spring and fall— and his family and guests enjoy perfectly barbecued foods all year around. The Weber Portable Table-Top Grill and Smoky Joe Kettles can go right along with mobile families, too. Pack them up on snow-mobiles, in station wagons, on pack horses, in canoes. However you travel you can take along the most important part of the meal—the Weber Kettle.

When you want to spend your time enjoying the great outdoors—be they snow-covered or spring-green—make the meal burgers and sausages. You'll please every taste. Burger makings, sausages and fixings can be packed at home, or you can stop at a market en route to pick up beef, franks, buns, catsup, cheese, pickles, etc. Don't forget the coffee. Take along hot spiced cider or wine for pre-dinner warmer-uppers.

Other party ideas begin with Weber-barbecued burgers and sausages. A Creativity Contest awards a bottle of wine to the guest who comes up with the most unusual, but edible, array of toppings for his burger or sausage. (Based on the assortment that you've put out, of course.)

Mark the first day of Spring with an impromptu neighborhood Burger-Fest. Feed the kids from one Kettle-full, then let the grown-ups have a second, more peaceful, sitting.

When it comes to entertaining teen-agers, there's only one place to do it—outside! And nothing matches their appetites better than Weber-barbecued sausages and burgers with the wildest assortment of "works" possible.

Bevy of Burgers page 33, Grilled Sausage page 34

SUPPER FOR THE WINTER SPORTS CROWD

MENU

Hot Spiced Cider, Sangria or Glogg
(carry to the cook-out in vacuum bottle or jug)
Cheese Ball with Assorted Fancy Crackers

A BEVY OF BURGERS
Page 33
French Fries, *Page 67*   OR   Potato Chips
Fancy Breads or Buns
(butter and wrap in foil to heat in a hurry at cook-out site)
Assorted Relishes

Red Wine (Optional)

FRUIT KABOBS
Page 70
OR
CHERRIES JUBILEE
Page 71

Coffee   Dessert Wine (Optional)

BACKYARD PARTY FOR TEEN-AGERS OR YOUNG ADULTS

MENU

Cheese Tray
Popcorn, Pretzels or Potato Chips
Chilled Soft Drinks or Chilled Root Beer

BURGERS AND SAUSAGE LINKS
With Fixings, *Pages 33-35*

POTATO SALAD
Page 65
Assorted Relishes and Pickles   Sliced Tomatoes
Hot Buttered Buns
Ice Cream Cones or Make-Your-Own Sundaes

Lemonade Coolers, *Page 75*
Iced Tea, *Page 75*   Soft Drinks

HAMBURGERS

They top every food preference poll

Everybody loves hamburgers. Fixed the Weber way they're handsomely browned, juicy and tender. Burgers can be economical, easy to cook and quick to fix. Dress them up with the "works" or keep them simple. Either way, they're great eating!

What Meat To Use— How Much To Buy?

Dinner-size, thick or rare burgers are best made with freshly ground lean chuck, round or sirloin tip. If possible, have the meat trimmed of excess fat and ground just once.

Hamburger, often a "special" at meat counters, makes fine traditional in-bun burgers to serve with all the trimmings.

One pound of raw meat will make 2 to 3 dinner-size patties or 3 to 4 patties to serve in buns.

Burger Cooking Chart— Charcoal Or Gas Kettles

Burger Thickness	Minutes per Side		
	Rare	Medium	Well Done
¾-inch	3	4	5
1-inch	4 to 5	5 to 6	6 to 7

STEAK BURGERS

CHARCOAL—DIRECT METHOD
GAS—INDIRECT METHOD HIGH HEAT

2 pounds ground lean chuck, round or sirloin tip
3 tablespoons finely chopped onion
2 teaspoons salt
¼ teaspoon black pepper
Favorite butter or basting sauce (page 62)

Combine first 4 ingredients; mix well. Shape into 6 to 8 patties ¾-inch thick. Refrigerate until ready to cook. Arrange patties on cooking grill. Cover kettle and cook until brown and crisp on underside. Turn, cover kettle and cook to doneness desired. Serve on toasted and buttered hamburger buns or bread. Yield: 6 to 8 burgers.

If you prefer to sear . . . Leave cover off 1 minute before cooking first side. Cover, cook, turn. Leave cover off 1 minute to sear second side, cover and cook.

ON GAS KETTLE: INDIRECT METHOD HIGH HEAT. Place patties in center area; cover and cook on 1st side. Turn and move to outer area of cooking grill. Cover and cook to desired degree of doneness (see cooking chart for approximate time).

If you prefer to sear. . . . Sear 1 minute on each side DIRECT METHOD HIGH HEAT. Move meat to outer area of cooking grill and switch to INDIRECT METHOD HIGH HEAT. Cover, cook on 1st side. Turn meat moving back into center area of cooking grill. Cover and cook to desired degree of doneness.

DINNER-SIZE STEAK BURGERS

Follow recipe for Steak Burgers; shape into 4 to 6 patties 1-inch thick. Yield: 4 to 6 servings.

BUDGET BURGERS

Follow recipe for Steak Burgers using ground chuck, round or hamburger and adding ¾ cup uncooked rolled oats and ½ cup tomato juice or milk to meat before mixing and shaping into patties. Prepare as directed for Steak Burgers. Serve on toasted and buttered hamburger buns or bread. Yield: 6 to 8 burgers.

DINNER-SIZE BUDGET BURGERS

Follow recipe for Budget Burgers; shape into 4 to 6 patties 1-inch thick. Yield: 4 to 6 burgers.

GENOESE BURGERS

Prepare Steak or Budget Burgers (page 32). Shape into 6 to 8 patties and cook as directed. Just before removing burgers from grill, top each with a slice of Provolone cheese and sprinkle with oregano; cover kettle and cook just long enough to soften cheese. Place burgers on bottoms of toasted buttered buns. Top each with chopped green onion, a tomato slice and a slice of Kosher or garlic dill pickle. Cover with bun tops. Yield: 6 to 8 burgers.

A BEVY OF BURGERS

BACONY CHEESEBURGERS

Prepare Steak or Budget Burgers (page 32). Shape into 6 to 8 patties and cook as directed. Before removing from grill top each hot burger with a slice of American or Swiss cheese and tomato. Cover kettle and cook just long enough to soften cheese. Top tomato slices criss-cross fashion with 2 crisp-cooked half slices of bacon. Serve on toasted and buttered whole wheat or rye hamburger buns. Yield: 6 to 8 burgers.

BURGUNDY BURGERS

Prepare Budget Burgers (page 32), substituting ¼ cup Burgundy wine for ¼ cup of the tomato juice or milk. Shape into 6 to 8 patties and cook as directed. Serve on toasted buns with Barbecue or Bearnaise Sauce (page 60). Yield: 6 to 8 burgers.

CALIFORNIA BURGERS

Prepare Steak or Budget Burgers (page 32). Shape into 6 to 8 patties and cook as directed. Peel and mash ½ avocado; fold in ¼ cup finely diced fresh tomato, 2 tablespoons finely chopped green onion, 2 teaspoons lemon juice and salt and pepper to taste. Slice remaining half avocado crosswise. Place patties on bottoms of toasted buns; top with avocado mixture. Garnish each burger with an avocado slice; cover with bun top. Yield: 6 to 8 burgers.

FAR EAST BURGERS

Prepare Steak or Budget Burgers (page 32). Before mixing meat add ¼ cup honey, 1½ to 2 teaspoons curry powder and ½ teaspoon *each* of cinnamon and ginger; mix and shape into 4 to 6 dinner-size patties and cook as directed. Combine ⅔ cup catsup, ½ cup orange juice, 3 tablespoons honey and 2 teaspoons cornstarch; mix. Cook until thickened, stirring constantly. Spoon sauce over cooked burgers; top each with an orange slice, an avocado slice and a halved strawberry or maraschino cherry. Yield: 4 to 6 dinner-size burgers.

MADRID BURGERS

Prepare Steak or Budget Burgers (page 32). Before mixing meat, stir in 1 teaspoon prepared mustard, ½ garlic clove, crushed, ½ teaspoon basil and 12 medium pimiento stuffed olives, finely chopped. Shape into 6 to 8 patties and cook as directed. Brush patties during cooking with olive oil, if desired. Arrange patties on bottoms of toasted and buttered hamburger buns. Top with catsup, finely chopped stuffed olives and bun tops. Yield: 6 to 8 burgers.

ROQUEFORT BURGERS

Prepare Steak or Budget Burgers (page 32). Before mixing meat, stir in 3 ounces of crumbled Roquefort or blue cheese. Shape into 6 to 8 patties and cook as directed. Place patties on slices of black bread spread with butter or margarine and prepared mustard. Top each with dollop of sour cream and second slice of black bread. Yield: 6 to 8 burgers.

MUSHROOM BURGERS

Prepare Steak or Budget Burgers (page 32). Before mixing meat add 1 can (2½ ounces) drained and chopped mushrooms, 2 tablespoons finely chopped green pepper and ¼ teaspoon Worcestershire sauce; mix well. Shape into 6 to 8 patties and cook as directed. Serve in buttered toasted hamburger buns with favorite barbecue sauce. Yield: 6 to 8 burgers.

TACO BURGERS

Prepare Steak or Budget Burgers (page 32). Before mixing meat, add ½ package (1¼ ounces) taco seasoning and ¼ cup catsup; mix. Shape into 6 to 8 patties and cook as directed. Top each patty with an American cheese slice 1 minute before end of cooking time; cover kettle and cook just long enough to soften cheese. Place each patty on toasted hamburger bun; top with chopped head lettuce and a tomato slice. Cover with bun top. Yield: 6 to 8 servings.

EVEN MORE BURGER TOPPINGS

Serve hot burgers on buttered toasted hamburger buns or other bread with one of the following toppings:

Combine and mix ½ cup dairy sour cream, 2 tablespoons finely chopped green onion or chives, 1 tablespoon prepared mustard and ¼ teaspoon fines herbes blend.

Arrange a slice of Mozzarella cheese on each hot burger; sprinkle with dried dill weed. Add a thin slice of sweet Spanish onion; cover with 1 or 2 thin slices of dill pickle and catsup, as desired.

Combine and mix ½ cup dairy sour cream, ¼ cup crumbled blue cheese and 1 tablespoon chopped pimiento.

Omit bun; arrange each burger on crisp round tortilla. Spoon a small amount of hot canned chili con carne with beans over burgers. Top each burger with finely chopped onion and lettuce; cover with thin tomato slice. Sprinkle with shredded Cheddar cheese and top with 1 or 2 hot chili peppers.

Spread each burger with mayonnaise. Cover with thin cucumber and radish slices. Season with salt and pepper; top with thin tomato wedges.

Top each burger with a thin tomato slice, a dollop of mayonnaise, well-drained sweet pickle relish and crisp lettuce.

Cover each burger with well-drained coleslaw, a sprinkling of caraway seed and thin slices of garlic dill pickle.

Spread each bun with catsup and prepared mustard. Top each burger with a grilled onion, Swiss cheese and tomato slice.

Spread each burger with mayonnaise; top with a thin slice of tomato and 1 or 2 thin wedges of avocado. Cover with lettuce.

Cover bottom of buns with drained sauteed sliced fresh or drained canned mushrooms. Add burger and cover with Bearnaise Sauce (page 60) or mayonnaise.

SAUSAGES
Popular cook-out meats

There's an almost endless variety of sausages, fully-cooked and uncooked, available for cook-out meals —just pick one to please your taste. Franks, wieners and hot dogs are everyone's favorites. They are relatively inexpensive and quick to heat and serve eager eaters.

Most favorite sausages are now available in two forms: *fully-cooked,* ready to heat and eat, and *uncooked,* requiring a thorough cooking before eating. Read the package label carefully, it describes the sausage and the cooking required.

Feature a variety of sausages at your next cook-out along with franks for the youngsters. You'll find that many guests enjoy the distinctive flavor of Bratwurst, Thuringer, smoked sausage links, ring bologna, etc.

GRILLED FULLY-COOKED SAUSAGE LINKS
Bratwurst, Smoked Sausage, Italian and Polish Sausage Links, Knackwurst, Ring Bologna, Franks, Weiners or Hot Dogs, etc.

CHARCOAL—DIRECT METHOD
GAS—INDIRECT METHOD HIGH HEAT

Preheat gas grill on DIRECT HIGH HEAT then turn to INDIRECT HIGH HEAT. Arrange links on well-greased cooking grill. Cover kettle and cook about 6 to 8 minutes or until links are hot and lightly browned. Turn links with tongs every 2 minutes.

GRILLED COOK-BEFORE-EATING SAUSAGE LINKS

CHARCOAL—INDIRECT METHOD
GAS—INDIRECT METHOD LOW HEAT

Brown sausages on cooking grill over coals at side of charcoal kettle or in gas kettle with cover off using DIRECT METHOD HIGH HEAT. Turn sausages with tongs as needed to brown evenly. Switch gas ketlte to INDIRECT METHOD LOW HEAT and place a drip pan in center of grill over lava rocks. Transfer meat to center of gas or charcoal grill. Cover kettle, cook 20 to 25 minutes or until done.

PORK SAUSAGE LINKS

CHARCOAL—INDIRECT METHOD
GAS—INDIRECT METHOD HIGH HEAT

Arrange sausage links on cooking grill over drip pan. Cover kettle and cook 18 to 25 minutes, depending upon size of link. Turn links with tongs at least once during cooking.

BROWN AND SERVE PORK SAUSAGE LINKS

CHARCOAL—DIRECT METHOD
GAS—INDIRECT METHOD HIGH HEAT

Preheat gas kettle on DIRECT METHOD HIGH HEAT then turn to INDIRECT METHOD HIGH HEAT. Center links on cooking grill; cover and cook 6 to 8 minutes, turning sausages with tongs 2 or 3 times during heating.

GRILLED SAUSAGE WHEELS

CHARCOAL—DIRECT METHOD
GAS—DIRECT METHOD LOW HEAT

Make slashes ½-inch apart in franks or smoked sausage links cutting almost to but not quite through bottom. Skewer ends of link together with wooden picks. Arrange sausages on well-greased cooking grill. Cover kettle and heat until lightly browned, turning once with long handled pancake turner. If desired, brush with Barbecue Sauce (page 60) during last few minutes of heating.

CHEESE FRANKS

CHARCOAL—INDIRECT METHOD
GAS—INDIRECT METHOD LOW HEAT

Slit franks lengthwise almost in half and to within ¼-inch of each end. Stuff the slit in each frank with shredded Cheddar cheese or folded American cheese slices. Brush with barbecue sauce or spoon on pickle relish. Wrap each frank in a slice of bacon; fasten with wooden picks. Center franks on cooking grill; cover kettle and cook 15 to 20 minutes or until bacon is crisp.

Cheese Franks page 35

fish and seafood

MENU

Chilled Melon With Proscuitto
Favorite Fruit, Vegetable or Clam Juice Cocktail
Fancy Assorted Crackers

CLAM BAKE
(Lobster Tails, Clams, Corn, Potatoes, *Page 40*)
Lemon Butter, *Page 62*
OR
WHOLE RED SNAPPER
Page 41
Weber's Cocktail Sauce, *Page 61*
Dilled Carrots, *Page 66*

TOSSED VEGETABLE SALAD
French or Russian Dressing
Hot Dinner Rolls, *Page 56*
OR
Hot Corn Bread Squares
Butter
Assorted Fresh Fruits   OR   Chilled Melon Wedges

Pound Cake

Coffee

LOBSTER DINNER

MENU

BROILED LOBSTER TAILS
Page 40
Lemon Butter, *Page 62*
OR
BROILED WHOLE LOBSTERS
Page 40
Lemon Butter, *Page 62*

Baked or French Fried Potatoes, *Page 67*
Broccoli Polonaise, *Page 66*

CAESAR SALAD
Page 65
Brown 'N Serve Rolls, *Page 56*

Peachy-Berry Cobbler, *Page 71*

Coffee

Whole Red Snapper page 41

FISH FOR BARBECUING

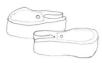

FISH STEAKS
Cut large fish such as salmon, sablefish, king mackerel, halibut, etc. into 1 to 1½-inch thick crosswise slices.

FISH FILLETS
Cut whole sides of fish from head to tail along either side of backbone and right next to cavity bones. The fillets should be scaled. Some fillets can be skinned, some may have skin left on. Lake trout, whitefish, snapper, yellow perch and many more fillets are available. Clean, wash, dry and cook.

DRESSED OR PAN-DRESSED FISH
Rainbow or brook trout, yellow or ocean perch and cat fish are readily available either fresh or frozen.

FISH PORTIONS AND STICKS
Boneless fish is shaped into sticks or squares and breaded. These ready-to-cook fish pieces are convenient and inexpensive.

WHOLE FISH
Must be scaled, drawn, washed and dried before cooking. Head, tail and fins may be removed, if desired. Salmon, red snapper, striped bass, trout and whitefish, as well as small pan fish, are all excellent for cooking whole.

A Few Cooking Hints

Make sure fish is top quality and FRESH! Clean quickly and refrigerate at once.

Lean fish is best for grilling—it holds its shape. Baste often while cooking.

Fish is very tender and cooks quickly.

Fish tends to break apart and stick to grill or pan. Be sure pan, grill or foil is well-greased. Skin tears easily so handle carefully.

Fish is done when it flakes easily with a fork. DO NOT OVERCOOK!

Rainbow Trout page 39

WHOLE LAKE TROUT OR OTHER LARGE FISH

CHARCOAL—INDIRECT METHOD
GAS—INDIRECT METHOD LOW HEAT

6 to 10-pound lake trout or other large fish
Salad oil
Lemon Butter or Basting Sauce (page 62)
Salt
Pepper
Dry mustard
Sweet basil
Lemon slices
Toasted sliced almonds

Make an aluminum foil pan large enough to hold fish. Brush surface of foil pan well with oil. Cut head and tail from fish, if desired. Clean fish, drain and dry with paper towels. Place fish on pan. Brush cavity with Lemon Butter or Basting Sauce. Sprinkle with salt, pepper, mustard and sweet basil. Brush outside of fish with Lemon Butter or Basting Sauce. Arrange lemon slices in row down top of fish; position fish in pan on cooking grill. Cover kettle; cook about 1 hour 45 minutes or until thickest part of fish flakes easily with fork. Brush with Lemon Butter or Basting Sauce several times during cooking. Sprinkle with toasted almonds. Yield: 6 to 10 servings.

BARBECUED FISH STEAKS

CHARCOAL—INDIRECT METHOD
GAS—INDIRECT METHOD LOW HEAT

6 individual salmon, halibut or other fish steaks
    ¾ to 1-inch thick, fresh or frozen
⅓ cup catsup
⅓ cup melted butter, margarine or oil
¼ cup lemon juice
2 tablespoons vinegar
1 tablespoon minced onion
2 teaspoons prepared mustard
1½ teaspoons salt
1 teaspoon Worcestershire sauce
1 teaspoon grated lemon peel
½ teaspoon paprika
1 small clove garlic, crushed
3 to 4 dashes hot red pepper sauce

Thaw frozen steaks. Arrange steaks in shallow baking pan. Combine remaining ingredients; mix. Pour over fish; refrigerate 30 minutes, turning steaks once. Drain fish, reserving sauce. Arrange steaks on well-greased shallow baking pan; brush with sauce. Place pan on cooking grill. Cover kettle and bake 8 to 10 minutes; carefully turn steaks and brush with sauce. Bake an additional 6 to 10 minutes or until fish flakes with a fork. Baste with sauce several times during cooking. Serve with any remaining sauce. Yield: 6 servings.

RAINBOW TROUT OR OTHER SMALL FISH COOKED IN FOIL

CHARCOAL—INDIRECT METHOD
GAS—INDIRECT METHOD LOW HEAT

Clean and dry 8 to 12-ounce dressed rainbow or brook trout, salmon or cat fish. Place about 1 tablespoon butter or margarine in cavity of each fish. Sprinkle cavity with lemon juice, salt and pepper. Brush outside of fish with oil. Place a strip of bacon lengthwise down both sides of each fish and wrap each fish in a double thick sheet of heavy duty aluminum foil. Seal edges securely. Arrange foil packages on cooking grill; cover kettle and cook 6 to 7 minutes. Turn packages with tongs and cook on second side 6 or 7 minutes or until fish flakes with a fork. Serve with Lemon Butter (page 62). Yield: 1 fish per serving.

SALMON STEAKS WITH LEMON BUTTER SAUCE

CHARCOAL—INDIRECT METHOD
GAS—INDIRECT METHOD LOW HEAT

6 salmon steaks, 1-inch thick, fresh or frozen
    (about 2 pounds)
Lemon Butter or Basting Sauce (page 62)

Thaw frozen steaks. Place fish in well-greased shallow pan or aluminum foil tray. Brush with Sauce. Place on cooking grill. Cover kettle and cook about 7 minutes. Carefully turn fish; baste with Sauce and cook 7 to 10 minutes longer or until fish flakes with a fork. Yield: 6 servings.

HICKORY SMOKED FISH STEAKS

CHARCOAL—INDIRECT METHOD
GAS—INDIRECT METHOD LOW HEAT

2 pounds salmon, halibut or other fish steaks,
    ¾ to 1-inch thick, fresh or frozen
Oriental Marinade (page 59)
2 teaspoons liquid smoke
Weber's Cocktail Sauce or Lemon Butter or Basting
    Sauce (pages 61 and 62)

Thaw frozen steaks. Cut into serving size portions; arrange in a single layer in shallow baking dish. Combine marinade and liquid smoke; pour over fish and refrigerate 30 minutes to 1 hour, turning pieces 1 or 2 times. Drain fish, reserving marinade for basting. Place fish in well-greased shallow baking pan. Place on cooking grill. Cover kettle; cook about 12 minutes, or until fish flakes easily with fork. Baste with reserved marinade 2 or 3 times during cooking. Serve with Weber's Cocktail Sauce or Lemon Butter or Basting Sauce. Yield: About 6 servings.

SHRIMP

CHARCOAL—DIRECT METHOD
GAS—INDIRECT METHOD LOW HEAT

2 pounds fresh or thawed frozen raw shrimp
1½ cups butter or margarine
Garlic salt or powder as desired
Lemon juice (optional and to taste)
Weber's Cocktail Sauce (page 61)

Make an aluminum foil pan large enough to hold shrimp 1 layer deep, or use a 10 x 15 x 1-inch jelly roll pan. Peel, devein and clean shrimp. Melt butter or margarine; stir in garlic salt or powder and lemon juice as desired. Arrange shrimp in pan. Pour seasoned butter over shrimp; center pan on cooking grill. Cover kettle and cook 5 to 8 minutes or until pink and firm, turning shrimp once. Time will vary depending on size of shrimp. Do not overcook! Serve with Weber's Cocktail Sauce. Yield: About 4 entrée servings, 6 to 8 appetizer servings.

BROILED LOBSTER TAILS

CHARCOAL—INDIRECT METHOD
GAS—INDIRECT METHOD LOW HEAT

8-ounce frozen lobster tails, thawed
Melted butter or margarine
Lemon wedges

Remove swimmerettes and sharp edges from tails. Cut off thin undershell membrane and any bony material with kitchen scissors. Wash and dry. Bend shell backward to crack shell. Brush tails with melted butter; place on cooking grill, shell side down. Cover kettle and cook 10 minutes. Brush with melted butter; cover kettle and cook 10 minutes or until shell is bright red. Serve with lemon wedges and additional melted butter. Yield: Allow 1 or 2 lobster tails per person.

BROILED WHOLE LOBSTERS

CHARCOAL—DIRECT METHOD
GAS—DIRECT METHOD LOW HEAT

Select live spiny, rock or northern lobsters, weighing ¾ to 1-pound each. To kill lobster instantly, lay it on its back and insert the tip of a sharp knife between body shell and tail segment; sever spinal cord. If preferred, insert tip of knife in center of small cross at back of head. Arrange lobsters on cooking grill shell side up. Cover kettle and cook 18 to 20 minutes or until shell is a bright red color. To serve, split lobster in half lengthwise, remove stomach (small sac) behind head and intestinal vein running down the center. Crack the claws. Serve with lemon wedges and melted butter or Lemon Butter (page 62). Yield: Allow 1 lobster per person.

CLAM BAKE

CHARCOAL—INDIRECT METHOD
GAS—INDIRECT METHOD LOW HEAT

18 lobster tails (3 ounces each)
3 dozen steamer clams
1 dozen small onions (about 1½ inches in diameter)
1 dozen small potatoes (about 2 inches in diameter)
6 ears corn
Melted butter or margarine
Lemon or lime wedges

Thaw frozen lobster tails. Cut away sharp edges, swimmerettes and undershell with kitchen scissors. Scrub clam shells thoroughly. Peel onions. Scrub potatoes; do not pare. Husk corn, remove silk; break ears in half. Cut 6 pieces of double thick cheesecloth and 6 pieces of double thick heavy duty aluminum foil, 18 x 24 inches each. Spread a piece of cheesecloth over each piece of foil. Arrange 3 lobster tails, 6 clams, 2 onions, 2 potatoes and 2 pieces of corn in center of each sheet of cheesecloth and foil. Tie opposite corners of cheesecloth together with string. Bring foil up over food. Pour 1 cup of water over food in each package and close package securely with a double fold at all edges. Place packages on cooking grill. Cover kettle. Cook for 50 to 60 minutes or until onions and potatoes are done. Serve with melted butter or margarine and lemon or lime wedges. Yield: 6 servings.

SMOKED FISH

CHARCOAL—INDIRECT METHOD
GAS—INDIRECT METHOD LOW HEAT

6 fish fillets (1 pound each) or small dressed
  fresh or frozen whole fish (rainbow trout,
  cat fish, etc.)
4 quarts water
1 cup salt
1 pound hardwood or hickory chips
2 cups water
⅓ cup salad oil

Thaw frozen fish and clean as needed. Measure 4 quarts water into large pan; add salt and stir until dissolved. Soak chips in 2 cups fresh water 20 minutes; drain and reserve to sprinkle over coals for smoking. Arrange fish 1 layer deep in flat pans; add salt water to cover generously. Refrigerate about 40 minutes. Drain fish well; rinse with cold water. Dry fish with paper towels. Sprinkle chips over coals or lava rock. Brush fish with oil; drain and arrange skin side down on cooking grill over drip pan. Adjust dampers or heat control knob to maintain low even temperature. Cover kettle and smoke about 35 to 40 minutes for fish 1-inch thick, 30 to 35 minutes for fish ¾ to 1-inch thick, 20 to 30 minutes for fish ½ to 1-inch thick or until fish is lightly browned and flakes with a fork. Briquettes may be added to charcoal kettle as needed to maintain heat; chips may be added as needed to produce smoke. Brush fish often with oil to keep it moist. Yield: About 6 servings.

WHOLE RED SNAPPER, SALMON, TROUT OR SEA BASS

CHARCOAL—INDIRECT METHOD
GAS—INDIRECT METHOD LOW HEAT

8 to 10-pound red snapper or other large fish
Melted butter, margarine or salad oil
½ cup lemon juice
1 tablespoon Worcestershire sauce
1 tablespoon prepared mustard
½ teaspoon basil
½ teaspoon garlic salt
½ teaspoon salt
1 medium onion, thinly sliced
1 lemon, thinly sliced

Make an aluminum foil pan large enough to hold fish. Brush surface of foil pan well with melted butter, margarine or oil. Cut head and tail from fish, if desired. Clean fish, drain and dry with paper towels. Place fish on pan. Combine lemon juice, Worcestershire sauce, prepared mustard, basil and salts; mix and brush in cavity of fish. Arrange ½ of the onion and lemon slices in a row in cavity of fish. If desired, stuff fish with Mushroom Stuffing (page 23) or Pecan or Almond Stuffing (page 45) or prepared packaged stuffing. Brush outside of fish generously with melted butter, margarine or oil. Overlap remaining onion and lemon slices down top of fish. Position fish in pan on cooking grill. Drizzle remaining lemon juice mixture evenly over fish. Cover kettle; cook 1½ to 1¾ hours, or until thickest part of fish flakes easily with fork. Do not turn fish during cooking. Yield: 8 to 10 servings.

SOFT SHELL CRABS

CHARCOAL—INDIRECT METHOD
GAS—INDIRECT METHOD LOW HEAT

16 dressed soft shell blue crabs, fresh or frozen
⅔ cup salad oil
⅓ cup minced parsley
2 tablespoons lemon juice
½ teaspoon soy sauce
2 dashes hot red pepper sauce
Lemon wedges

Thaw frozen crabs; clean, wash and dry. Combine oil, parsley, lemon juice, soy sauce and hot pepper sauce; mix. Center crabs on well-greased cooking grill over a drip pan or in well-greased large shallow foil pan on cooking grill. Brush crabs with sauce. Cover kettle; cook 7 to 8 minutes. Brush crabs with sauce; turn with tongs and brush with sauce again. Cover kettle and cook 6 to 10 minutes or until crabs are lightly browned. Serve with lemon wedges. Yield: 8 servings.

poultry

Turkey means holidays or feasting to most of us. But turkeys are relatively inexpensive and, with a Weber Kettle, more than relatively easy to roast. So don't wait for the next big holiday on the calendar to enjoy a golden-brown, juicy and fragrant big bird!

Or how about a chicken in every kettle? Moderately priced broiler-fryers or fryers are always popular, and the flavor that comes from cooking them on a Weber Charcoal or Gas Kettle makes them taste very expensive. You can flavor whole chickens, halves or pieces with marinades, sauces or butters or basting sauces (pages 59-62). Only a computer could figure out the number of variations possible!

Turkey makes an occasion special, and chicken is an every-day classic, but don't forget other members of the poultry family. Duck, with its incomparable flavor and juiciness, barbecues beautifully, especially when brushed with a fruited basting sauce. Rock Cornish Hens allow each guest a whole bird. (Why not serve them for a Henry VIII party?) Capons are extra-heavy, extra-meaty chickens. Roasted in a Weber Kettle they surpass memories of Grandma's roast chicken. For real convenience, try one of today's frozen boneless turkey rolls—a real boon to the cook who loves to barbecue but hates to carve a bird. Complete instructions for roasting turkey rolls are in this chapter, or follow package directions.

CHICKEN OR CAPON DINNER

Chicken every Sunday?
With a Weber Kettle chicken is so good you'll
be tempted to serve it every day!

MENU

Avocado or Onion Dip*   OR   Liver Pâté*
Assorted Crackers
Favorite Fruit or Vegetable Cocktail

ROASTED CHICKEN OR CAPON
Page 47
Fruited or Almond Rice
Green Beans, Curried Sour Cream, *Page 66*
Minted Peas, *Page 67*

FRUIT SALAD IN MELON BOWL
Page 64
OR
Your Own Fruit Salad
Hot Biscuits or French Bread   Butter

PEACHY-BERRY COBBLER
Page 71

Coffee   Tea   Lemonade Coolers, *Page 75*

*Available in specialty food stores or gourmet shops.

FAMILY OR HOLIDAY TURKEY DINNER

Turkey cooked the Weber way makes
any meal an occasion.

MENU

Hot Shrimp Appetizers, *Page 40*
Favorite Fruit or Vegetable Cocktail

ROASTED TURKEY
Page 44
Pecan Stuffing, *Page 45*   Turkey Gravy
Mashed Potatoes
Cranberry Glazed Sweet Potatoes, *Page 73*
Green Beans Amandine, *Page 66*

CRANBERRY ORANGE SALAD
Page 64
Hot Rolls   Butter

PUMPKIN PIE

Coffee   or   Tea

Turkeys Cooked The Weber Covered Kettle Way

Any turkey roasts to perfection in a Weber Cooking Kettle. Try fresh or thawed frozen turkeys, stuffed or unstuffed, or thawed frozen turkey rolls.

What Size Turkey To Buy?

Unstuffed fresh and thawed frozen turkeys (6 to 24-pounds) are excellent for roasting in Weber Charcoal or Gas Kettles. Turkey size depends on the number of guests and the size of your Weber Kettle.

Size Turkeys Available

Six to 12-pound turkeys are available most of the year. Order larger turkeys a few days ahead of the big meal.

Turkey Rolls

Frozen boneless turkey rolls (2 to 10-pounds) are easy to roast and carve. Small rolls (2 to 5-pounds) are usually available; larger ones (5 to 10-pounds) should be ordered a few days ahead.

How Much Oven-Ready Turkey To Buy?

Cut	Serving allowance per person (raw weight)
Boneless turkey roll	1/3 to 1/2 pound
Unstuffed turkey	
6 to 12 pounds	3/4 to 1 pound
13 to 24 pounds	1/2 to 1 pound

BARBECUED TURKEY ROLL

CHARCOAL—INDIRECT METHOD
GAS—INDIRECT METHOD LOW HEAT

Thaw frozen turkey roll (page 45). Tie roll securely with heavy string every 1½ inches or follow package directions. Center roll on cooking grill over drip pan. Cover kettle and cook until fork tender or meat thermometer reaches an internal temperature of 175°F. Baste with favorite barbecue or basting sauce (pages 60-62) during last 20 minutes of cooking. Yield: About 2 servings per pound.

ROASTED UNSTUFFED TURKEY

(Stuffed turkeys take more time to cook. Stuffing can be baked separately in a casserole along with turkey the last 45 minutes of roasting.)

CHARCOAL—INDIRECT METHOD
GAS—INDIRECT METHOD LOW HEAT

Oven-ready turkey
Salt
Pepper
Salad oil, melted butter or margarine

Clean turkey; sprinkle cavities generously with salt and pepper. Lock wings behind back or fasten next to breast and tie securely; tie legs and tail together securely or press legs under band of skin. Insert meat thermometer into thickest portion of thigh with point away from bone. Center turkey on greased cooking grill or in roast holder on cooking grill directly over drip pan. Brush with oil, melted butter or margarine. Cover kettle; cook to 185°F. Add briquettes as needed to maintain temperature. If stuffed turkey is desired allow 3 to 5 minutes additional cooking time per pound. See Turkey Cooking Chart, next page, for approximate cooking times.

PECAN OR ALMOND
BREAD STUFFING

¾ cup butter or margarine
1 cup diced celery
¾ cup finely chopped onion
5 cups ½-inch cubes day-old bread
½ cup hot water
1 egg, beaten
3 teaspoons poultry seasoning
½ cup chopped pecans or toasted almonds
1½ teaspoons salt
¼ teaspoon pepper

Melt butter or margarine in large skillet. Add celery and onion; cover and cook slowly until onion is tender, not brown. Remove from heat. Add remaining ingredients; toss lightly. Excellent for chicken, Rock Cornish hens, capon, duck or goose. For turkey, turn stuffing into casserole and bake along with turkey last 45 minutes of roasting. Yield: About 6 cups.

How To Thaw Frozen Unstuffed Turkey Or Boneless Turkey Roll

Follow manufacturer's directions on casing, bag or label to thaw frozen turkey or rolls, or see below.

To thaw turkey, leave in original casing and
1.) thaw in pan in refrigerator; or,
2.) in a pan of cold water; or,
3.) in a pan under cold running water.

Cook at once or refrigerate no longer than 24 hours before cooking. NEVER REFREEZE!

IMPORTANT! *Never* thaw turkeys at room temperature or in warm water. Use thawed turkeys quickly. *Never* store a thawed turkey in refrigerator for more than 24 hours. *Never* refreeze!

Turkey Cooking Chart—
Charcoal Or Gas Kettles

Fresh or thawed frozen ready-to-cook Pounds	Cook to internal temperature of (°F.)	Approximate total cooking time in hours
Unstuffed		
6 to 8	185	2 to 2¾
8 to 12	185	2½ to 3¾
12 to 16	185	3½ to 4
Boneless turkey roll		
2 to 5	175	1½ to 2
5 to 10	175	2 to 3½

For stuffed turkeys, allow about 3 to 5 minutes more per pound.

Approximate Thawing Time For Frozen Unstuffed Turkeys Or Turkey Rolls

Turkey Weight (Pounds)	Thawed In	It will take
8 to 12	Refrigerator	1 to 2 days
8 to 12	Cold water and refrigerator	8 to 10 hours in cold water to soften then 4 to 6 hours in refrigerator.
12 to 20	Refrigerator	2 to 3 days

How Much Stuffing Will You Need?

For	Weighing (Pounds)	Cups of Stuffing Needed (About)
Capon	5 to 6	6
Chicken	4	4
Rock Cornish hens	¾ to 1	¾ to 1 per hen
Duck	3½ to 5	4 to 5
Goose	10 to 12	10 to 12 (2½ to 3 quarts)
Turkey	7 to 8	8
	10 to 12	10 to 12 (2½ to 3 quarts)
	16	16
	20 to 24	20 to 24 (5 to 6 quarts)

BARBECUED TURKEY PIECES

CHARCOAL—INDIRECT METHOD
GAS—INDIRECT METHOD LOW HEAT

Cut a 6 to 8-pound thawed turkey into serving pieces. Prepare as directed for Bar-B-Q Chicken (page 47). Turkey pieces are larger and will take longer to cook than chicken. Yield: 8 to 10 servings.

CHICKEN PIECES, QUARTERS OR HALVES A LA LASHER

CHARCOAL—INDIRECT METHOD
GAS—INDIRECT METHOD LOW HEAT

3-pound fryer, cut into pieces, quarters or halves
1½ teaspoons salt
⅛ teaspoon pepper
Melted butter, margarine or favorite basting or
   barbecue sauce (page 60 or 62)

Rinse pieces of chicken with cold water; pat dry with paper towel. Season chicken with salt and pepper. Arrange chicken pieces, skin side up, on cooking grill over drip pan. Brush with melted butter, margarine or basting sauce. Cover kettle and cook about 1 hour or until tender. After 30 minutes brush chicken with melted butter, margarine or basting sauce. Baste 2 or 3 times during cooking. Yield: 2 to 4 servings.

PARMESAN CHICKEN KEMPSTER

CHARCOAL—INDIRECT METHOD
GAS—INDIRECT METHOD LOW HEAT

1 cup crushed herb-seasoned stuffing mix
⅔ cup grated Parmesan cheese
¼ cup finely chopped parsley
2½ to 3-pound broiler-fryer, cut into serving pieces
½ cup butter or margarine, melted

Combine stuffing mix, cheese and parsley. Dip chicken pieces in melted butter or margarine; roll in stuffing mixture. Arrange chicken pieces, skin side up, in large well-greased shallow baking pan. Drizzle any remaining butter or margarine over chicken; sprinkle with remaining crumbs. Center pan on cooking grill; cover kettle and cook about 1 hour 20 minutes or until chicken is fork tender. Yield: About 4 servings.

BAR-B-Q CHICKEN

CHARCOAL—INDIRECT METHOD
GAS—INDIRECT METHOD LOW HEAT

⅓ cup vinegar
¼ cup salad oil
¼ cup water
2 tablespoons Worcestershire sauce
1 tablespoon sugar
¾ teaspoon salt
½ teaspoon dry mustard
¼ teaspoon hot red pepper sauce
3 to 3½-pound fryer, cut into serving pieces

Combine and mix first 8 ingredients. Bring to a boil. Remove from heat; keep hot. Arrange chicken pieces on cooking grill. Cover kettle and cook about 1 hour or until fork tender, basting frequently with sauce. Yield: About 4 servings.

ROASTED CHICKEN

CHARCOAL—INDIRECT METHOD
GAS—INDIRECT METHOD LOW HEAT

3 to 3½-pound whole fryer
1½ teaspoons salt
⅛ teaspoon pepper
Melted butter, margarine or favorite basting
    sauce (page 62)

Wash chicken with cold water; pat dry with paper towel. Lock the wings behind back; tie legs together securely. Brush chicken with melted butter, margarine or basting sauce and sprinkle cavity with salt and pepper. Center chicken on greased cooking grill over drip pan. Cover kettle. Cook 1 hour and 30 minutes or until chicken is tender and lightly browned. Baste chicken with butter, margarine or basting sauce during last 30 minutes of cooking. Yield: 3 to 4 servings.

ROASTED CAPON

Follow recipe for Roasted Chicken at left and increase cooking time to 2 to 2¼ hours or until tender.

ROCK CORNISH HENS STUFFED WITH CHICKEN LIVERS

CHARCOAL—INDIRECT METHOD
GAS—INDIRECT METHOD LOW HEAT

4 Rock Cornish hens
¾ teaspoon salt
8 slices bacon
⅔ cup minced onion
½ pound chicken livers, chopped
½ cup butter or margarine, melted
4 slices white bread, torn into fine crumbs
½ teaspoon sage
¼ teaspoon pepper

Clean and dry hens. Sprinkle ¼ teaspoon salt in body cavities of all hens. Dice 4 strips of bacon. Sauté bacon pieces, onion and livers in ¼ cup butter or margarine until onion is tender. Add crumbs, remaining salt, sage and pepper; mix well. Stuff hens with bread mixture. Use wooden picks or small metal skewers and string to close cavity openings. Wrap a bacon strip around each hen; secure with wooden picks. Brush hens with remaining butter or margarine. Arrange hens on cooking grill over drip pan; cover kettle. Cook about 1 hour and 20 minutes or until done and golden brown. Brush hens with additional butter or margarine as needed during cooking. Yield: 4 servings.

ORANGE BURGUNDY DUCKLING

CHARCOAL—INDIRECT METHOD
GAS—INDIRECT METHOD LOW HEAT

1 5-pound duckling
1 cup Burgundy wine
1 teaspoon salt
¼ teaspoon pepper
¼ teaspoon thyme
1 orange, quartered
2 slices onion
1 washed celery top
½ can (6 ounces) thawed frozen orange juice
    concentrate

Brush cavity of duck with small amount of the Burgundy. Sprinkle cavity with salt, pepper and thyme. Stuff with orange quarters, onion slices and celery top; close cavity opening with skewers. Combine remaining Burgundy and orange juice concentrate; mix and brush outside of duck with mixture. Center duckling on cooking grill over drip pan. Cover kettle and roast 2 to 2¼ hours or until tender. After roasting 30 minutes prick skin in fatty areas with large needle and baste with wine-orange mixture. Baste frequently during roasting. Discard cavity contents before serving. Yield: About 4 servings.

CHARCOAL—DIRECT METHOD. Charcoal should be spaced apart in a sparse layer so heat is not too intense.

GAS—DIRECT METHOD LOW HEAT. CAUTION: When using the direct method, be careful to keep heat from getting too high.

Always Spectacular Food!

Kabob dinners, plain or fancy, are easy on the hostess and great fun for family and guests.

Every cook-out fan loves to spear an assortment of colorful tasty foods on a skewer and watch it sizzle until perfectly cooked.

Make Kabob Cooking Easy

Trim excess fat from meat to prevent flare-ups.

Leave meat, fish, seafood or poultry in serving size portions or cut into 1 to 1½-inch cubes, as desired.

Marinate meats, fish, seafood or poultry, if desired. Prepare marinade (page 59). Arrange food in a refrigerator dish or plastic bag; pour marinade over. Cover and refrigerate 2 to 4 hours, turning pieces 2 or 3 times

Prepare sauces, butters or basting sauces (pages 60-62).

Prepare kabob "go-with" foods (pages 50 and 51); cover and refrigerate until serving time.

Position and attach kabob rack to cooking grill. Heat Weber Kettle as directed on page 4 or 5.

Drain meat, fish, seafood or poultry well. Save marinade for basting, if desired.

Assemble trays or bowls of foods, sauces, skewers and other tools on table near Weber Kettle.

Cooking time determines skewer line-ups—thread 1 or 2 kinds of food that cook in about the same length of time onto skewers. Skewers of longer-cooking food go in the grill first.

Don't crowd food on skewers. Allow space for hot air to circulate. Use a square of green pepper or a small piece of fruit to hold foods apart.

Arrange skewers in kabob rack.

Brush foods with marinade or sauce (pages 59-62). If a very sweet or thick barbecue or fruit sauce is used brush it over foods during the last 5 to 8 minutes of cooking only, to avoid burning or over-browning.

Cook foods to desired doneness. Remember that pork must be cooked well-done—see chart on page 50.

IMPORTANT! Keep an eye on the kabobs while cooking. Baste as needed and turn as necessary to brown evenly.

Remove skewers from rack and transfer foods to serving platter or dinner plates.

FIX-YOUR-OWN KABOB PARTY

No need to plan entertainment for this party— the fun is in the fixing!

MENU

Fruit Juice or Other Cocktail
Hot Pastry Appetizers*
Tray of Weber Skewers

TRAY OF ASSORTED MEATS: BEEF CHUNKS, LAMB CHOPS, HAM CUBES AND SMALL LOBSTER TAILS

Bowls of Bacon-Wrapped Sweet Potato Quarters, Whole or Half Tomatoes, Green Pepper Squares, Canned or Partially Cooked Onions, Carrot Chips, Fresh Mushrooms and Cooked Artichoke Hearts

BOWLS OF FRESH OR CANNED PINEAPPLE, CANTALOUPE AND BANANA CHUNKS, LEMON, LIME OR ORANGE SLICES

Barbecue Sauce, *Page 60*
Buttered Rice with Chives and Parsley

RED APPLE SALAD
Page 63

Hot Rolls   Butter   Assorted Relishes

CHERRIES JUBILEE
Page 71

Iced or Irish Coffee

*May be found in frozen food cases in fine grocery stores or supermarkets.

Lamb-Vegetable Kabobs page 51

Kabob Food Combinations

Marinade recipes page 59.
Sauce recipes pages 60 and 61.
Butter and basting sauce recipes page 62.

MEAT	USE	CUT INTO	GO-WITH VEGETABLES	GO-WITH FRUITS

BEEF	Sirloin
	Tenderloin
	U.S. Prime or Choice
	  chuck or
	  tenderized round
		1 to 1½ -inch
		cubes
			Fresh mushroom caps
			1-inch green pepper
			  squares or strips
			Small canned or precooked
			  potatoes and/or onions
			Brussels sprouts
				Fresh or canned
				  pineapple
				Canned cling peach
				  halves, cut in half
				Spiced crab apples

HAM AND HAM-LIKE PRODUCTS	Boneless fully-cooked
	  ham
	Canadian bacon or
	  canned minced ham or
	  luncheon meat
		1 to 1½ -inch
		cubes
			Canned or parboiled fresh
			  sweet potato chunks
			Thick slices of zucchini
			1-inch green pepper squares
			Tomato quarters
				Chunks of fresh
				  pineapple, cantaloupe
				  or honeydew melon
				Thick banana slices
				Spiced crab apples
				Watermelon pickle
				  pieces
				Lime or orange chunks

PORK	Boneless shoulder
	Loin or Tenderloin
	
	NOTE: Fresh pork must be well-cooked before eating. Cook with foods that are done in the same time as pork. If preferred sauté pork until tender and lightly browned before threading onto skewers.
		¾ to 1¼ -inch
		cubes
			Acorn squash squares
			2-inch lengths of corn on cob
			Water chestnuts
			Canned sweet potato
			  chunks wrapped in bacon
				Same as for ham and
				  ham-like products
				  above

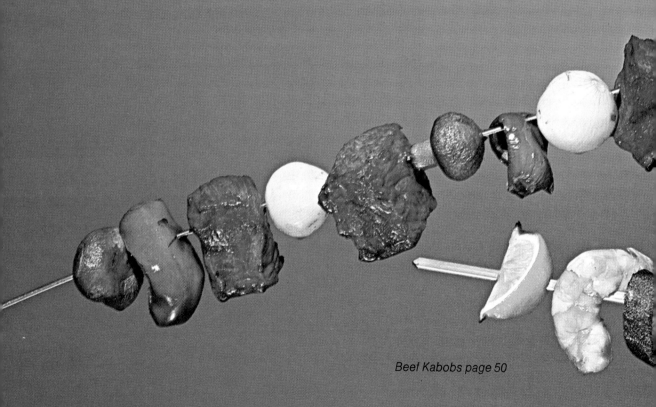

Beef Kabobs page 50

MEAT	USE	CUT INTO	GO-WITH VEGETABLES	GO-WITH FRUITS
LAMB	Boneless leg of lamb Boneless shoulder or boneless rib or loin chops	1 to 1½-inch cubes 1 or 2-rib chops	Any of vegetables listed under ham	Any of fruits listed under ham or beef
SAUSAGE—FULLY-COOKED	Franks, Bratwurst, Knackwurst, smoked sausage links or brown and serve pork sausage	Crosswise into 1½ to 2-inch lengths	Any of the vegetables listed under ham	Any of fruits listed under ham
FISH AND SEAFOOD	2 to 4 oz. lobster tails Shrimp Scallops Salmon, halibut, etc.	Clean; leave whole Cleaned and deveined Cut into 1½-inch cubes	Tomato halves or quarters Zucchini slices Same as for beef	Unpeeled lemon or orange quarters

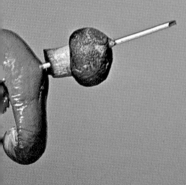

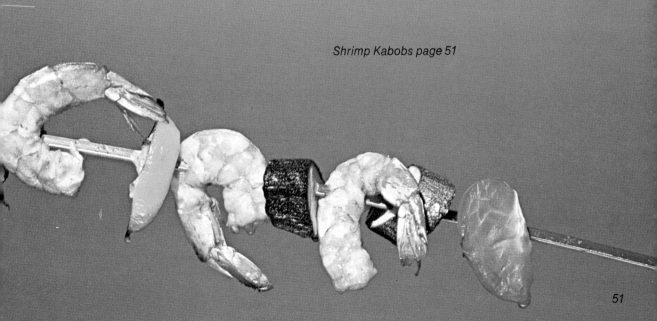

Shrimp Kabobs page 51

51

wok cooking

CHINESE DINNER

*You and your Weber Wok can produce an honorable
meal to rival any beyond the Great Wall!*

MENU

HOT CHINESE EGG ROLLS
With Chinese Mustard or Sweet Sour Sauce*

CHICKEN WITH WALNUTS
Page 55

OR

SUKIYAKI
Page 54

OR

SHRIMP
WITH CHINESE PEA PODS
Page 55

Almond or Steamed Rice
Assorted Preserved Fruits or Pickles (Kumquats
Watermelon, Ginger, Orange Wedges,
Sweet or Sour Pickles)*
Spears of Romaine

CHILLED MELON SLICE
OR
PINEAPPLE SHERBET
Almond or Fortune Cookies*

Tea

*Available in Chinese or gourmet food shops.

Chinese cooks do wonderful things with foods in the versatile Wok. The centuries-old Wok is a spherical bottomed pan designed for stir-fry or chow cooking, but it can also be used as a skillet, saucepan or steamer. Wok cooking requires very high heat and foods cook to perfection in just a few minutes.

The Weber Wok is large enough to stir and toss foods with plenty of space to pull foods up on the sides of the pan while other foods cook.

Just a few tricks make stir-fry cooking safe, easy and fun.

Before using, wash Wok with hot sudsy water. Rinse with hot water and dry well. Rub inside surface with cooking oil, then wipe off excess oil with paper toweling.

Prepare all foods in advance. Have all chopping, slicing, mixing etc. done *before* heating Wok. Once cooking starts it goes very quickly! Pack each food in a plastic bag or covered bowl; refrigerate until ready to cook.

Assemble all needed tools and foods within easy reach of Weber Kettle: Long handled shovel and ladle, long handled brush, asbestos gloves, serving dishes and foods.

Remove cover and cooking grill. Heat Wok. The brackets on the underside of the Wok are positioned to fit Gas Units and 18½ and 22½'' Weber Kettles.

TO HEAT WEBER CHARCOAL KETTLE
Place 120 to 150 briquettes in a pyramid shape in center of charcoal (lower) grill (see drawing at left). Heat briquettes until covered with gray ash. Set Wok in place making sure that Wok nestles in coals. Proceed as recipe directs.

TO HEAT WEBER GAS KETTLE
Follow directions on page 5 DIRECT METHOD. Set Wok in place and proceed as recipe directs. Heat may be adjusted as needed.

IMPORTANT! Once cooking has started, NEVER leave the Wok! Stir-fry foods cook in minutes and need constant attention!

Cool Wok and clean after each use. See directions for cleaning above. After cleaning Wok should be coated with cooking oil to prevent rust.

Shrimp with Chinese Pea Pods page 55

SWEET-SOUR PORK

CHARCOAL—DIRECT METHOD
GAS—DIRECT METHOD HIGH HEAT

Sweet-Sour Sauce:
¼ cup cornstarch
⅔ cup each of:
    water, cider vinegar, pineapple juice and
    firmly-packed brown sugar
3 tablespoons catsup
2 tablespoons soy sauce

Meat:
3 tablespoons salad oil
3 pounds lean boneless pork shoulder or
    tenderloin, cut in 1-inch cubes
1 cup warm water
½ cup thinly sliced carrot
1 medium onion, halved and thinly sliced
1 can (1 pound 4 ounces) pineapple chunks,
    drained
1 medium green pepper, cleaned and cut in 1-inch
    squares
1 medium tomato, peeled and cut in ¼-inch wedges
½ cup well-drained pickled melon chunks
    (watermelon rind or cantaloupe)
6 cups hot cooked seasoned rice or almond rice

Prepare Sauce: Add cornstarch to small saucepan. Stir in remaining sauce ingredients. Mix well; cook until smooth and thickened, stirring constantly. Cover and reserve. Heat oil in Wok; brush on sides of pan. Add ¼ of pork cubes at a time and stir constantly until meat is browned; pull up on sides of Wok where heat is lower. Repeat until all meat is browned. Return meat to center of pan; add warm water. Cover Wok. Simmer 15 minutes. Add more water if needed. Add carrot slices and cook 15 minutes longer or until pork is done. Add onion; cook and stir until onion is limp. Stir in reserved sauce. Fold in pineapple chunks, green pepper, tomato wedges and melon pickles. Heat, stirring constantly. Serve with rice. Yield: About 8 servings. To serve 4, cut recipe in half.

SUKIYAKI

CHARCOAL—DIRECT METHOD
GAS—DIRECT METHOD HIGH HEAT

2 pounds lean boneless top grade sirloin,
    tenderloin or tenderized round, cut ½-inch thick
2 beef bouillon cubes, crushed
1 cup boiling water
⅓ cup soy sauce
⅓ cup dry sherry or sake
2 teaspoons sugar
½ teaspoon salt
Dash of black pepper
1 pound spinach, washed, leaves cut in half or
    quarters
2 cups diagonally sliced (1-inch) celery cabbage
    or 1½ cups diagonally sliced (¾-inch) celery
1½ cups green onion slices (2-inch), cut in half
    lengthwise
1 can (1 pound) bean sprouts, rinsed and drained
½ pound fresh mushrooms, washed and sliced
1 cup green pepper squares (1-inch)
1 can (5 ounces) sliced bamboo shoots, drained
2 tablespoons cornstarch
½ cup cold water
¼ cup salad oil
6 to 8 cups hot cooked seasoned rice

For easier slicing freeze beef until partially frozen. Cut beef across grain into thin slices (⅛-inch or less); cut slices 2 inches long. Dissolve bouillon cubes in boiling water; stir in soy sauce, sherry or sake, sugar, salt and pepper; reserve. Prepare vegetables; keep separate and refrigerate if not preparing Sukiyaki at once. Combine cornstarch and cold water; mix and set aside. Heat oil in Wok; brush on sides of pan. Brown meat quickly in hot oil, stirring constantly until well browned. Pull meat up sides of Wok where heat is lower. Add vegetables; cook and stir 2 or 3 minutes. Add broth mixture; heat, stirring constantly. Stir in cornstarch mixture; cook and stir constantly until sauce is thick and clear and vegetables hot, yet crisp. Serve at once with hot rice. Yield: 8 to 10 servings. For 4 servings cut recipe in half.

CHICKEN WITH WALNUTS

CHARCOAL—DIRECT METHOD
GAS—DIRECT METHOD HIGH HEAT

1 cup walnut halves
3 tablespoons butter or margarine
3 large whole chicken breasts, skinned and boned
2 tablespoons cornstarch
2 teaspoons sugar
1½ teaspoons salt
3 cups canned chicken bouillon
3 tablespoons soy sauce
½ cup salad oil
1 package (10 ounces) frozen cut green beans,
    thawed
2 cups diagonally sliced (½-inch) celery
1 can (8½ ounces) sliced bamboo shoots, drained
1 can (8 ounces) water chestnuts, drained and
    thinly sliced
4 cups hot cooked seasoned rice

Sauté walnuts in butter or margarine in skillet until lightly browned. Drain walnuts on paper towels; reserve. Cut chicken into thin julienne strips; reserve. Combine and mix cornstarch, sugar and salt. Blend in 1 cup chicken bouillon and soy sauce; stir until smooth and reserve. Heat oil in Wok; brush on sides of pan. Sprinkle chicken into oil; cook and stir until chicken turns white and browns slightly. Stir in vegetables. Pour remaining 2 cups of chicken bouillon over mixture; cover and steam about 5 minutes. Remove cover; stir in cornstarch mixture and continue cooking and stirring until sauce is thick and clear. Add walnut halves and heat, stirring constantly. Serve with hot cooked seasoned rice. Yield: 6 servings.

SHRIMP WITH CHINESE PEA PODS

CHARCOAL—DIRECT METHOD
GAS—DIRECT METHOD HIGH HEAT

2 tablespoons cornstarch
1 teaspoon sugar
½ teaspoon salt
1 cup canned chicken bouillon
1 tablespoon soy sauce
3 tablespoons salad oil
2 pounds cooked, peeled and deveined medium
    shrimp, fresh or frozen, thawed
2 packages (7 ounces each) frozen Chinese pea
    pods, thawed (or 2½ cups fresh Chinese pea
    pods)
1 can (8 ounces) water chestnuts, drained and
    thinly sliced
¾ cup diagonally sliced (½-inch) celery
½ cup diagonally sliced (1-inch) green onion
6 cups hot seasoned cooked rice

Combine cornstarch, sugar and salt; mix. Stir in bouillon and soy sauce; mix until smooth and reserve. Heat oil in Wok; brush on sides of pan. Add shrimp and cook, stirring constantly until hot. Pull shrimp up on sides of Wok where heat is lower. Add vegetables to oil, a few at a time. Cook, stirring constantly until vegetables are thoroughly heated and tender, yet crisp. Mix shrimp with vegetables; cook and stir until hot. Stir cornstarch-bouillon mixture into Wok; cook, stirring constantly until sauce thickens. Serve at once with hot rice. Yield: 8 servings. If 4 servings are desired, cut recipe in half.

breads

FRENCH OR ITALIAN BREAD IN FOIL

CHARCOAL—INDIRECT METHOD
GAS—INDIRECT METHOD LOW HEAT

Cut bread crosswise into 1-inch slices, cutting to but not quite through bottom crust. Spread cut surfaces with softened butter or margarine. Wrap loaf in double thick heavy duty aluminum foil; seal with double fold on top and ends. Center on cooking grill; cover kettle and heat 15 to 20 minutes. For a crisp crust loosen foil on top and ends 5 minutes before end of heating time.

VARIATIONS

Prepare French or Italian bread as directed above except omit butter or margarine and spread bread with one of the following mixtures.

CARAWAY CHEESE FRENCH BREAD . . . Combine and mix 1 cup shredded process American cheese, ½ cup *each* of softened butter or margarine and salad dressing and 2 tablespoons caraway seed.

GARLIC BREAD . . . Combine and mix ½ cup softened butter or margarine, ¼ cup grated Parmesan cheese, 1 crushed garlic clove and ¼ teaspoon *each* of marjoram and oregano.

HERB BREAD WITH BLUE CHEESE . . . Combine and mix 1 cup softened butter or margarine, 4 ounces blue cheese, crumbled, 2 teaspoons *each* of chopped parsley and instant minced onion and 1 teaspoon *each* of rosemary and basil.

HERBED GARLIC BREAD . . . Combine and mix ½ cup soft Garlic Butter (page 62), 1 tablespoon finely chopped parsley, ¼ teaspoon *each* of basil and oregano and a dash of pepper.

SWISS CHEESE LOAF . . . Combine and mix 1 cup shredded Swiss cheese, ⅓ cup softened butter or margarine and ¼ cup *each* of finely chopped onion and chili sauce.

HOT DINNER ROLLS AND SANDWICH BUNS

CHARCOAL—INDIRECT METHOD
GAS—INDIRECT METHOD LOW HEAT

Cut baked dinner rolls (hard or soft), hamburger or hot dog buns in half; spread cut surfaces with softened butter or margarine or a favorite seasoned butter (page 62). Wrap 4 to 6 rolls or buns in double thick heavy duty aluminum foil; seal with double fold on top and ends. Heat as directed for French or Italian Bread.

BROWN 'N SERVE ROLLS

CHARCOAL—INDIRECT METHOD
GAS—INDIRECT METHOD LOW HEAT

Remove rolls from package; break apart. Brush tops and bottoms of rolls with melted butter or margarine. Wrap in heavy duty aluminum foil; seal with double fold on top and ends. Center on cooking grill; cover kettle and heat 8 to 10 minutes, or until hot and lightly browned.

MARMALADE ROLLS

CHARCOAL—INDIRECT METHOD
GAS—INDIRECT METHOD LOW HEAT

Separate rolls in 1 package (12 rolls) brown 'n serve dinner rolls. Cut each roll through center, not quite to bottom. Arrange rolls in well-buttered muffin pans. Brush tops with melted butter or margarine. Spread 1 to 1½ teaspoons marmalade or preserves (orange, pineapple, red raspberry, strawberry or apricot) in each cut. Center on cooking grill; cover kettle and bake 8 to 10 minutes or until rolls are hot and lightly browned. Yield: 12 rolls.

SWEET ROLLS

CHARCOAL—INDIRECT METHOD
GAS—INDIRECT METHOD LOW HEAT

Wrap 2 to 6 sweet rolls loosely in double thick heavy duty aluminum foil. Heat as directed for Hot Dinner Rolls (page 56).

HOT CARAMEL ROLLS

CHARCOAL—INDIRECT METHOD
GAS—INDIRECT METHOD LOW HEAT

Melt ¼ cup butter or margarine; add ¼ cup firmly-packed light brown sugar and heat slowly until sugar melts. Separate 1 package (12 rolls) brown 'n serve rolls; butter 12 muffin cups. Place one roll in each cup. Spoon an equal amount of butter-brown sugar syrup over each roll and tuck in 2 or 3 pecan halves. Center on cooking grill; cover kettle and bake about 15 minutes or until rolls are hot and lightly browned.

DILLY BREAD

CHARCOAL—INDIRECT METHOD
GAS—INDIRECT METHOD LOW HEAT

Combine and mix ⅓ cup melted butter or margarine, 2 tablespoons *each* of chopped parsley and lemon juice and ½ teaspoon dried dill weed. Separate rolls in 2 packages (8 ounces each) refrigerated biscuits; dip each biscuit into dill butter. Stand biscuits upright on edge in greased 5½-cup ring mold. Brush top with remaining dill butter. Center pan on cooking grill; cover kettle and bake 15 to 18 minutes or until done and lightly browned. Serve hot. Yield: About 10 servings.

YEAST BREAD

CHARCOAL—INDIRECT METHOD
GAS—INDIRECT METHOD LOW HEAT

Prepare 1 or 2 loaves of yeast bread from favorite recipe or hot roll or bread mix. Brush inside of aluminum foil loaf pan (or pans) with butter or margarine. Brush loaves of bread lightly with melted butter or margarine just before baking. To bake, center pan (or pans) on cooking grill; cover kettle and bake 35 to 40 minutes depending upon size of pan or until done and nicely browned. Cool on rack 5 minutes. Remove from pan (or pans); finish cooling on rack. Brush with melted butter or margarine while hot.

QUICK NUT BREAD

CHARCOAL—INDIRECT METHOD
GAS—INDIRECT METHOD LOW HEAT

2 cups unsifted flour
¾ cup sugar
1 teaspoon baking soda
1 teaspoon baking powder
1 teaspoon salt
1 cup dairy sour cream
½ cup butter or margarine, softened
2 eggs
1 teaspoon vanilla
1 cup chopped walnuts

Combine ingredients in order listed in large mixer bowl. Mix at low speed until blended. Pour into well-greased 9 x 5 x 3-inch loaf pan. Center on cooking grill; cover kettle and bake 60 to 65 minutes or until cake tester inserted in center of loaf comes out clean. Cool 10 minutes. Remove from pan; finish cooling on rack. Yield: One 9 x 5 x 3-inch loaf.

appetizers

CHA SHEW
Chinese Red Pork

CHARCOAL—INDIRECT METHOD
GAS—INDIRECT METHOD LOW HEAT

2 pounds whole pork tenderloin (about 1½ inches
   in diameter)
1½ teaspoons red food coloring
1 teaspoon seasoned salt
½ cup pineapple juice
½ cup honey
⅓ cup soy sauce
⅓ cup sherry
⅓ cup finely chopped preserved ginger
¼ cup preserved ginger syrup
2 tablespoons cornstarch

Brush tenderloins with red food coloring; sprinkle
with seasoned salt. Place in roast holder in foil pan;
cover lightly with aluminum foil. Center on cooking
grill; cover kettle and roast 1¼ to 1½ hours, or until
fork tender. Combine and mix remaining ingredients
in saucepan; cook, stirring constantly, until thick and
clear. Brush meat with a small amount of sauce 2 or
3 times during last 15 minutes of cooking. Slice meat
very thin; serve hot or cold with remaining sauce for
dipping. Garnish with fresh pineapple or honeydew
melon slices, if desired. Yield: About 10 to 12
servings.

Cha Shew page 58

BACON CRAB ROLLS

CHARCOAL—INDIRECT METHOD
GAS—INDIRECT METHOD LOW HEAT

8 slices bacon, cut in half crosswise
1 package (6 ounces) thawed frozen crab meat,
   drained, boned and flaked
½ cup finely torn soft bread crumbs
1 teaspoon finely chopped onion
2 tablespoons salad dressing
1 teaspoon lemon juice
½ teaspoon prepared mustard

Cook bacon until half done, not crisp. Drain slices on
paper towel. Combine crab meat, crumbs and onion;
mix well. Combine salad dressing, lemon juice and
mustard; add to crab meat and mix well. Shape into
16 small rolls; wrap each in a half slice of bacon and
secure with wooden pick. Arrange in shallow baking
pan. Center on grill; cover kettle and cook about 4
to 5 minutes or until bacon is brown and crisp and
filling hot. Turn as needed to brown evenly. Yield:
16 appetizers.

GRILLED PORK OR BEEF APPETIZERS À LA GEIMER

CHARCOAL—INDIRECT METHOD
GAS—INDIRECT METHOD LOW HEAT

¼ cup soy sauce
2 tablespoons salad oil
½ teaspoon sugar
⅛ teaspoon cinnamon
1 clove garlic, crushed
2 dashes hot red pepper sauce
Dash of ground cloves
1 pound lean pork tenderloin or beef sirloin,
   cut into bite-size thin strips
1 small fresh pineapple, peeled and cut in
   bite-size chunks
1 medium green pepper, cleaned and cut in
   squares (¾-inch)

Combine first 7 ingredients in bowl; mix. Add meat;
mix. Cover and refrigerate about 2 hours, stirring 2
or 3 times. Drain meat, reserving marinade. String
meat, pineapple and green pepper on heavy bamboo skewers. Arrange on cooking grill over drip pan;
cover kettle and cook 5 to 10 minutes for beef and
10 to 15 minutes for pork, or until meat is done, basting with marinade during cooking. Turn 2 or 3 times.
Protect hand with asbestos glove before turning
kabobs. Yield: About 6 servings.

LAMB MARINADE

Combine and mix 1 cup dry red wine, ½ cup salad or olive oil, 1 tablespoon minced parsley, 2 teaspoons salt, 1½ teaspoons curry powder, 1 teaspoon dry mustard, ¼ teaspoon pepper and 1 crushed clove of garlic. Pour over 3 cups sliced onion and 1 cup chopped green pepper. Use leftover marinade for basting sauce. Yield: About 4½ cups marinade, enough for 3½ to 4 pounds lamb cubes.

ORANGE-SHERRY MARINADE

For pork, ham, ribs or poultry

Combine and mix 1 cup orange juice, ⅔ cup sweet sherry, ¼ cup vinegar, ¼ cup orange marmalade, 2 tablespoons minced parsley, 1 teaspoon basil and ¾ teaspoon salt. Use leftover marinade for basting sauce. Yield: About 2 cups.

ORIENTAL MARINADE

For poultry, seafood, beef, pork, ribs, ham or lamb

Combine and mix ½ cup *each* of soy sauce, salad oil and sherry or sake with ⅓ cup pineapple or lemon juice, ¼ cup drained chopped chutney (if desired), 2 crushed small cloves of garlic, 2 tablespoons sugar and 1 teaspoon *each* of ginger and salt. Use leftover marinade for basting sauce. Yield: About 2 cups.

STEAK MARINADE

For beef or lamb

Combine 1 cup tarragon or cider vinegar, ⅔ cup salad oil, ½ medium onion (thinly sliced), 1 teaspoon salt, 3 cloves garlic (thinly sliced), 8 peppercorns, 1 teaspoon *each* of basil and leaf thyme or oregano. Use leftover marinade for basting sauce. Yield: About 1¾ cups marinade.

SWEET AND SOUR MARINADE

For pork, ham, ribs or poultry

Combine and mix 1 cup pineapple juice, ½ cup *each* of lemon juice and red wine, ½ cup sliced green onion, 1 tablespoon Worcestershire sauce, 1 teaspoon leaf thyme, ¾ teaspoon salt, ½ teaspoon rosemary and ¼ teaspoon pepper. Use leftover marinade for basting sauce. Yield: About 2¼ cups.

WEBER KABOB MARINADE

For beef, lamb, poultry, pork, ham or seafood

Combine and mix 1 cup soy sauce, ½ cup *each* of wine or cider vinegar, pineapple juice and firmly-packed light brown sugar, 2 teaspoons salt and ½ teaspoon garlic powder. Use leftover marinade for basting sauce. Yield: About 2⅓ cups.

How To Marinate

The Easy Efficient Way

Arrange food in plastic food bag; place in flat pan and pour marinade into bag. Close bag securely with metal tie strip, rubber band or string. Turn bag over once or twice to coat food with marinade. Refrigerate for time recommended in specific recipe, turning bag several times.

The Old Fashioned Way

Layer food and marinade in refrigerator dish or bowl. Cover and refrigerate for time recommended in specific recipe, turning food several times.

HERB-WINE MARINADE

For beef, pork, lamb or fish

Combine and mix 1 cup dry red wine, ⅔ cup salad oil, 2 crushed cloves of garlic, ½ lemon (thinly sliced), 2 teaspoons minced parsley, 1 teaspoon *each* of leaf thyme and basil, ½ teaspoon salt and ¼ teaspoon pepper. Use leftover marinade for basting sauce. Yield: About 1⅔ cups marinade.

LEMON MARINADE

For fish, seafood, poultry or lamb

Combine and mix ⅔ cup fresh lemon juice, ¼ cup cider vinegar, ¼ cup salad oil, 2 tablespoons minced onion, 1 tablespoon minced parsley, ¾ teaspoon salt, ½ teaspoon grated lemon peel and ¼ teaspoon *each* of white pepper and paprika. Use leftover marinade for basting sauce. Yield: About 1 cup.

sauces

WEBER'S TANGY BARBECUE SAUCE

½ cup chopped celery
3 tablespoons finely chopped onion
2 tablespoons butter or margarine
1 cup catsup
¼ cup lemon juice
2 tablespoons each of vinegar and sugar
1 tablespoon Worcestershire sauce
1 teaspoon dry mustard
¼ teaspoon salt
Dash pepper

Cook celery and onion in butter until tender but not brown. Stir in all remaining ingredients; simmer 10 to 12 minutes. Yield: About 1½ cups.

BARBECUE SAUCE

For beef, pork, lamb, sausages, poultry or fish

Combine and mix in saucepan 1 cup catsup or chili sauce, ⅓ cup *each* of finely chopped onion and celery, ¼ cup *each* of cider vinegar, firmly-packed brown sugar and salad oil, 1 tablespoon Worcestershire sauce, ½ teaspoon salt and 2 or 3 dashes hot red pepper sauce. Simmer gently 8 to 10 minutes. Yield: About 2¼ cups.

BEARNAISE SAUCE

For meat, fish, seafood, vegetables or meat fondues

¼ cup cider or tarragon vinegar
¼ cup finely chopped onion
¼ cup water or dry white wine
1 tablespoon each of minced parsley and chives
3 egg yolks
½ cup butter or margarine
¾ cup salad dressing or mayonnaise
¼ teaspoon salt

Simmer vinegar and onion until liquid evaporates. Stir in water or wine, parsley and chives and set aside. Beat egg yolks until very thick and lemon-colored. Melt butter. Beat melted butter into egg yolks, a small amount at a time. Turn into heavy saucepan; cook over very low heat, stirring constantly, until thick. Remove from heat; stir in wine mixture. Fold in salad dressing and salt. Yield: About 2 cups.

B-B-Q SAUCE

For spareribs or short ribs

½ cup light molasses
½ cup catsup
½ cup chopped onion
⅓ cup orange juice
1 tablespoon shredded orange peel
1 tablespoon vinegar
1 tablespoon salad oil
1 tablespoon bottled steak sauce
1 tablespoon butter or margarine
½ teaspoon prepared mustard
½ teaspoon Worcestershire sauce
¼ teaspoon garlic powder
¼ teaspoon salt
¼ teaspoon pepper
¼ teaspoon hot red pepper sauce
3 whole cloves

Combine and mix ingredients in saucepan; bring to a boil over low heat. Simmer 5 minutes. Yield: About 2 cups.

WEBER'S COCKTAIL SAUCE

For fish or seafood

Combine and mix ½ cup catsup or chili sauce, 1 tablespoon *each* of horseradish and lemon juice and ¼ teaspoon salt. Yield: About ¾ cup.

CUMBERLAND SAUCE

For duck, goose, ham or spareribs

1 cup red currant jelly
⅔ cup orange juice
¼ cup lemon juice
2 teaspoons cornstarch
1 cup Port or Madeira wine
1 tablespoon grated orange peel
2 tablespoons Grand Marnier, optional

Combine first 3 ingredients in saucepan. Bring to a boil over low heat. Mix cornstarch and ¼ cup wine until smooth; slowly add to jelly mixture, stirring constantly. Cook and stir until mixture starts to thicken slightly; stir in remaining wine and orange peel. Stir in Grand Marnier just before serving. Yield: About 3 cups.

HOLLANDAISE SAUCE

For meat, fish, ham or vegetables

¾ cup butter or margarine
¼ teaspoon salt
Dash of cayenne
2 tablespoons lemon juice
3 egg yolks

Beat butter, salt and cayenne until soft and creamy. Beat in lemon juice, a few drops at a time. Add egg yolks, one at a time, beating after each addition until light and fluffy. Turn into top of double boiler. Beat over hot, not boiling, water for 2 to 3 minutes, until glossy. Remove from heat. Serve hot. Yield: About 1½ cups.

CREAMY MUSTARD SAUCE

For ham or vegetables

2 egg yolks, beaten
¼ cup water
2 tablespoons prepared mustard
1½ tablespoons vinegar
4 teaspoons sugar
1 teaspoon salt
⅛ teaspoon garlic salt
½ cup whipping cream

Combine first 7 ingredients in heavy saucepan; mix well. Cook over very low heat, stirring constantly, until mixture thickens, about 5 minutes. Remove from heat. Cool thoroughly. Whip cream and fold into mustard mixture. Yield: About 1⅓ cups sauce.

JAPANESE DIPPING SAUCE

For chicken, pork, ham, fish, seafood or kabobs

Combine and mix ¾ cup soy sauce, ½ cup *each* of lemon juice and dry sherry, ⅓ cup finely chopped drained preserved ginger, ¼ cup chopped green onion, 1 teaspoon grated fresh ginger or ¼ teaspoon ground ginger, ½ teaspoon sugar and ¼ teaspoon salt. Let stand 2 to 3 hours before using. Yield: About 2 cups.

ORANGE RAISIN SAUCE

To serve with ham, Canadian bacon or smoked pork shoulder

Combine ½ cup sugar, 1½ tablespoons cornstarch and ¼ teaspoon salt in saucepan; mix well. Stir in 1½ cups cold water and 1 can (6 ounces) frozen orange juice concentrate, thawed. Cook over low heat, stirring constantly, until sauce thickens. Stir in ⅓ cup seedless raisins; heat. Yield: About 2½ cups.

MEDIUM WHITE SAUCE

Melt 2 tablespoons butter or margarine in saucepan over low heat. Remove from heat; stir in 2 tablespoons flour, ½ teaspoon salt and dash of pepper. Stir in 1 cup milk; return to heat and cook slowly, stirring constantly, until thickened. Yield: About 1 cup.

SWEET-SOUR BARBECUE SAUCE

For pork, ribs, ham or poultry

1 can (8½ ounces) crushed pineapple
1 cup sugar
2 tablespoons cornstarch
½ teaspoon salt
⅔ cup cider or wine vinegar
⅓ cup coarsely chopped green pepper
¼ cup chopped maraschino cherries

Drain pineapple, reserving syrup. Add water to pineapple syrup, if necessary, to make ⅔ cup. Combine and mix sugar, cornstarch and salt in small saucepan; stir in pineapple syrup and vinegar. Cook slowly, stirring constantly, until thick and clear. Fold in pineapple, green pepper and maraschino cherries; heat. Yield: About 2⅔ cups.

butters

HERB BUTTER OR BASTING SAUCE

For pork, beef, lamb, fish, seafood, vegetables, rolls or bread

Combine and mix 1 cup softened or melted butter or margarine, 1 tablespoon minced parsley, 2 teaspoons minced onion, 1½ teaspoons fines herbes blend and ½ teaspoon onion salt. Yield: About 1 cup.

CHEESE AND PICKLE BUTTER SPREAD

For breads, rolls, steaks, burgers or fish

Combine and mix 1 cup softened butter or margarine with ¾ cup shredded Cheddar cheese, ¼ cup well-drained sweet pickle relish, 2 teaspoons *each* of minced onion and parsley and ¼ teaspoon seasoned salt. Yield: About 1¾ cups.

WINE-HERB BUTTER

For beef, pork, lamb, fish, seafood or poultry

Stir ⅓ cup dry white wine, a small amount at a time, into 1 cup softened butter or margarine; beating well after each addition. Stir in 1 tablespoon *each* of minced parsley, chives and fresh dill and 2 dashes hot red pepper sauce. Yield: About 1⅓ cups.

PARMESAN CHEESE BUTTER OR BASTING SAUCE

For steaks, burgers, breads, rolls or vegetables

Combine and mix 1 cup softened or melted butter or margarine, ⅓ cup grated Parmesan cheese, ⅓ cup minced onion and 1½ teaspoons oregano. Yield: About 1½ cups.

ROQUEFORT CHEESE SPREAD

For steaks or burgers

Fold ⅓ cup crumbled Roquefort or blue cheese and 2 teaspoons minced parsley into 1 cup softened butter or margarine. Yield: About 1¼ cups.

SHERRY MARMALADE BUTTER OR BASTING SAUCE

For poultry, pork, ham, ribs or kabobs

Combine and mix 1 cup softened or melted butter or margarine, ⅓ cup orange marmalade, ¼ cup sherry, 2 tablespoons drained finely chopped preserved ginger and 1 tablespoon *each* of soy sauce and lemon or orange juice. Yield: About 1⅔ cups.

APRICOT BUTTER OR BASTING SAUCE

For poultry, ham, pork, ribs or kabobs

Combine and mix 1 cup softened or melted butter or margarine, ¾ cup apricot preserves and 2 teaspoons grated orange or lemon peel. Yield: About 1¾ cups.

LEMON BUTTER OR BASTING SAUCE

For fish, seafood, poultry, vegetables or buns used for fish sandwiches

Combine and mix 1 cup softened or melted butter or margarine, ¼ cup lemon juice, 1 tablespoon minced parsley, ¾ teaspoon grated lemon peel and ¼ teaspoon salt. Yield: About 1¼ cups.

GINGER-CURRY BUTTER

For pork, ham, poultry, kabobs, roasts, chops or ribs

Combine and mix 1 cup softened or melted butter or margarine, ⅓ cup drained chopped preserved ginger, 2 tablespoons preserved ginger syrup, 1 tablespoon soy sauce, ¾ teaspoon curry powder and ¼ teaspoon salt. Yield: About 1½ cups.

ONION BUTTER OR BASTING SAUCE

For beef, vegetables, bread or rolls

Combine and mix 1 cup softened or melted butter or margarine, 1 envelope (1⅜ ounces) dry onion soup mix and 2 teaspoons minced parsley. Yield: About 1¼ cups.

GARLIC BUTTER OR BASTING SAUCE

For beef roasts, steaks, burgers, bread or rolls

Crush 2 small garlic cloves. Add to 1 cup softened or melted butter or margarine. Stir in 2 teaspoons minced parsley, ½ teaspoon marjoram and 4 dashes hot red pepper sauce. Yield: About 1 cup.

salads

RED APPLE SALAD

4 cups diced, washed, unpared red eating apples
1 cup drained pineapple tidbits
⅓ cup quartered maraschino cherries
1½ cups thinly sliced celery
½ cup coarsely chopped walnuts or peanuts
¾ cup salad dressing
2 tablespoons sugar
1 teaspoon lemon juice
⅛ teaspoon salt
½ cup whipping cream, whipped
Crisp salad greens

Combine fruits, celery and nuts in bowl. Combine and mix salad dressing, sugar, lemon juice and salt. Fold in whipped cream. Add to fruit; mix carefully. Chill until ready to serve. Serve on crisp salad greens. Yield: 6 to 8 servings.

BEAN SALAD

1 can (1 pound) kidney beans
1 can (1 pound) whole green beans
1 can (1 pound) cut wax beans
2 cups diced celery
½ cup finely chopped onion
½ cup finely chopped green pepper
⅔ cup vinegar
⅔ cup sugar
⅓ cup salad oil
⅓ cup water
1 teaspoon nutmeg
1 teaspoon salt
⅛ teaspoon pepper

Drain all beans well. Combine first 6 ingredients in bowl; mix carefully. Combine and mix remaining ingredients; pour over vegetables. Cover; chill 2 to 4 hours or overnight. Yield: About 6 servings.

FRUIT SALAD IN MELON BOWL

6 to 7-inch slice watermelon, cut from one end
1 small cantaloupe, peeled, seeded and cut into
    bite-size pieces
1 small honeydew melon, peeled, seeded and cut
    into bite-size pieces
1 cup fresh or canned drained pineapple chunks
1 cup orange or grapefruit segments
1 cup fresh strawberry halves
2 bananas, cut in ¾-inch slices
2 tablespoons lime or lemon juice
6 to 8 clusters sugar-frosted green or red
    grapes, optional

Cut a thin slice from end of watermelon so bowl will
stand upright and level. Cut red meat from inside of
watermelon leaving a 1-inch layer of red meat over
bottom. Cut scallops around top edge of watermelon
rind. Chill. Remove seeds from remaining watermelon; cut into bite-size pieces. Combine with fruits,
except grapes; mix carefully. Spoon into watermelon
shell. Arrange on serving plate; surround with sugar
frosted grapes, if desired. Yield: 10 to 12 servings.

HOT MACARONI DINNER SALAD

CHARCOAL—INDIRECT METHOD
GAS—INDIRECT METHOD LOW HEAT

6 slices bacon, diced
2 tablespoons vinegar
1 tablespoon chopped onion
½ teaspoon prepared mustard
1 teaspoon salt
¼ teaspoon pepper
1 package (7 ounces) elbow macaroni, cooked
    and drained
½ cup sliced radishes
¼ cup diced green pepper
¼ cup diced celery
¼ cup minced parsley

Fry bacon until crisp. Drain bacon on paper towel,
reserving 1 tablespoon drippings. Combine reserved
bacon drippings, vinegar, onion, mustard, salt and
pepper in skillet with long heatproof handle. Place on
cooking grill and heat until bubbly. Add macaroni
and bacon pieces; toss lightly and heat. Stir in remaining ingredients; heat. Yield: About 6 servings.

PINEAPPLE CREAM SALAD

2 packages (3 ounces each) lime-flavored gelatin
1 cup boiling water
1 pint (2 cups) dairy sour cream
½ teaspoon salt
1 can (1 pound) crushed pineapple, well-drained
½ cup finely chopped pecans
Crisp salad greens

Dissolve gelatin in boiling water; cool. Stir in sour
cream and salt. Chill until syrupy. Fold in pineapple
and nuts. Pour into 8 lightly oiled individual molds;
chill until firm. Unmold on crisp salad greens. Yield:
About 8 servings.

CRANBERRY ORANGE SALAD

2 packages (3 ounces each) orange-flavored gelatin
1 cup boiling water
2 cans (1 pound each) jellied cranberry sauce,
    mashed
¾ cup orange juice
2 teaspoons grated orange peel, optional
¾ cup chopped pared apple
⅔ cup finely diced celery
Crisp salad greens

Dissolve gelatin in boiling water. Add cranberry
sauce and orange juice; mix and cool. Stir in grated
orange peel; chill until mixture begins to set. Fold in
apple and celery. Pour into lightly oiled 5-cup mold
or individual molds. Chill until firm. Unmold on crisp
salad greens. Yield: About 8 servings.

SAUERKRAUT SALAD

⅓ cup vinegar
⅓ cup sugar
¼ cup salad oil
¼ teaspoon salt
1 can (1 pound) sauerkraut, rinsed and drained
1 cup finely chopped celery
1 small onion, finely chopped
½ medium green pepper, finely chopped
1 jar (2 ounces) pimiento, chopped
½ teaspoon caraway seed

Combine and heat vinegar, sugar, oil and salt until sugar dissolves. Pour over sauerkraut; stir in remaining ingredients. Cover; chill several hours or overnight. Yield: About 6 servings.

HOT GERMAN POTATO SALAD

CHARCOAL—INDIRECT METHOD
GAS—INDIRECT METHOD LOW HEAT

10 slices bacon, cut into ½-inch pieces
1 cup thinly sliced celery
¾ cup chopped onion
5 cups sliced cooked potatoes
¾ cup water
⅓ cup vinegar
3 tablespoons sugar
2 tablespoons flour
2 teaspoons salt
¾ teaspoon dry mustard
½ teaspoon celery seed
Dash of pepper
1 or 2 tablespoons chopped parsley

Fry bacon until crisp; drain on paper towel. Save ½ cup bacon drippings; pour into large skillet with long heatproof handle. Place on cooking grill. Add celery and onion; cook until tender, stirring constantly. Add potatoes; mix carefully. Combine and mix water, vinegar, sugar, flour, salt, dry mustard, celery seed and pepper. Pour over potato mixture; cook until liquid is thickened, stirring carefully as needed. Sprinkle bacon and parsley over top. Yield: About 8 servings.

CAESAR SALAD

¾ cup olive or salad oil
2 medium cloves garlic
1½ cups croutons
8 cups crisp torn salad greens (Romaine,
    Boston and/or Bibb lettuce)
2 tablespoons lemon juice
½ teaspoon salt
Freshly ground black pepper
2 eggs, coddled 1 minute
6 anchovy fillets, chopped
½ cup grated Parmesan cheese

Pour oil into small bowl. Crush 1 garlic clove in garlic press; add to oil. Let stand 30 minutes to 1 hour. Brown croutons slowly in ¼ cup of the garlic oil; cool. Cut remaining clove of garlic in half; rub salad bowl with garlic and discard. Toss salad at table or at cart near table. Turn greens into salad bowl. Sprinkle with lemon juice, salt and pepper. Pour remaining garlic oil over greens; toss lightly until leaves are evenly coated. Break eggs into salad; toss thoroughly. Add croutons, anchovies and cheese; toss gently. Serve at once. Yield: 10 to 12 servings.

POTATO SALAD FOR 25

25 medium potatoes, cooked, chilled, pared
    and sliced
3½ cups thinly sliced celery
1½ cups finely chopped Bermuda onion
1 cup chopped sweet pickles
6 hard-cooked eggs, chopped
4 cups salad dressing
1 cup French dressing
¼ cup chopped parsley
2 tablespoons salt
Leaf lettuce
Cherry tomatoes, optional

Combine first 5 ingredients in large mixing bowl; toss lightly. Add remaining ingredients except lettuce and tomatoes; mix carefully. Cover; refrigerate until serving time. Serve in lettuce lined bowl. Garnish with cherry tomatoes, if desired. Yield: About 6 quarts, 25 servings.

vegetables

Ways To Season Vegetables

Prepare fresh or frozen vegetables in aluminum foil as directed on page 67; season or serve as directed below.

ASPARAGUS

Amandine—Lightly brown ¼ cup slivered blanched almonds in 2 tablespoons butter or margarine. Stir in 1 tablespoon lemon juice. Pour over asparagus just before serving.

Hollandaise—Serve with favorite Hollandaise sauce (home-made or mix).

Parmesan—Sprinkle with grated Parmesan cheese just before serving.

Polonaise—Melt 3 tablespoons butter or margarine over low heat. Add ¼ cup fine dry bread crumbs; stir until crumbs are lightly browned. Chop 1 hard cooked egg. Top vegetable with crumbs, egg and chopped parsley.

Rolled Rump Roast page 12,
Corn and Potatoes page 68

BROCCOLI

Amandine
Hollandaise } Same as for asparagus
Polonaise

BEANS, GREEN OR WAX

Amandine—Same as for asparagus

Bacony—Mix in 2 or 3 tablespoons crisp cooked bacon bits and 1 tablespoon bacon drippings before serving.

Curried Sour Cream—Mix ½ cup dairy sour cream and ¼ teaspoon curry powder; warm over low heat. Stir into hot beans before serving.

CAULIFLOWER

Bacony—Same as for beans

Polonaise—Same as for asparagus

Curried Sour Cream—Same as for beans

CARROTS

Dilled—Add 2 tablespoons finely chopped onion and ¼ to ½ teaspoon chopped dried dill weed to carrots before closing package.

Sherry-Chive—Before serving stir 2 tablespoons sherry and 1 teaspoon chopped chives into carrots.

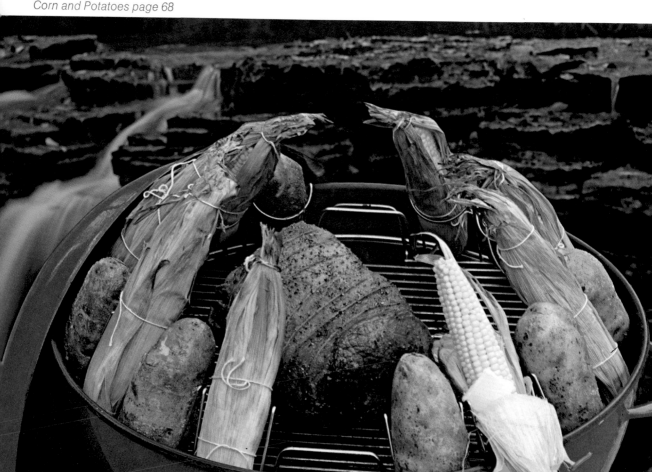

PEAS

Herbed—Sprinkle ½ teaspoon fines herbes blend over peas before closing package.

Minted—Sprinkle 1 teaspoon minced mint leaves over peas before closing package.

Mushroom—Add ¼ cup chopped fresh or canned mushrooms to peas before closing package.

ZUCCHINI

Italian—Sprinkle ½ to 1 teaspoon oregano over zucchini before closing package. Before serving sprinkle with 1 or 2 tablespoons grated Parmesan cheese.

FRESH VEGETABLES COOKED IN FOIL

CHARCOAL—INDIRECT METHOD
GAS—INDIRECT METHOD LOW HEAT

Center 2 or 3 servings of cleaned prepared vegetable on a 10 or 12-inch double thick square of heavy duty aluminum foil. Lift foil edges slightly. Season as desired with salt and pepper. Dot with 1 tablespoon butter or margarine or butter basting sauce. (page 62). Add 1 tablespoon water. Close package securely with a double fold on top and ends, leaving a little space for steam expansion. Place on cooking grill; cover kettle and cook until tender, turning package once. Prepare as many packages as needed. See chart below for approximate cooking times.

FROZEN VEGETABLES COOKED IN FOIL

(Except Creamed and Those Packed in Plastic Bags)

Thaw 9 or 10 ounce package of frozen vegetables until they can be broken apart. Center vegetables on a double thick 10 to 12-inch square of heavy duty aluminum foil. Proceed as directed for fresh vegetables above.

Vegetable Cooking Chart— Charcoal And Gas Kettles

(Foil Wrapped Packages)

Vegetable	Minutes	
	Fresh	Frozen
Artichoke Hearts	—	20 to 25
Asparagus Whole or 2-inch pieces	10 to 20	10 to 20

Vegetable	Minutes	
	Fresh	Frozen
Beans: Green, Italian, Wax Whole or in 1½-inch pieces	20 to 35	20 to 30
Broccoli Flowerets and stem, whole or 2-inch pieces	15 to 20	20 to 22
Brussels Sprouts	20 to 25	25 to 30
Carrots Sliced crosswise or quartered lengthwise	30 to 45	—
Cauliflower Flowerets	15 to 20	20 to 22
Corn Kernels	20 to 25	25 to 30
Eggplant Peeled and cut in 1-inch cubes	30 to 40	—
Mushrooms Whole or sliced	8 to 12	—
Peas Shelled	15 to 20	15 to 20
Peas and Carrots	—	15 to 20
Zucchini Sliced or quartered lengthwise	25 to 30	—

FROZEN POTATO PRODUCTS

CHARCOAL—INDIRECT METHOD
GAS—INDIRECT METHOD LOW HEAT

Spread ½ teaspoon butter or margarine in center of double thick 8 or 10-inch square of heavy duty aluminum foil. Center 1 serving of partially thawed French Fries, Potato Puffs, Potato Patties or Hash Browns on foil. Dot with ½ teaspoon butter or margarine. Season with salt and pepper. Close package securely with double fold at top and ends. Repeat as needed. Place on cooking grill; cover kettle and cook 15 to 18 minutes. Turn once during heating.

POTATOES BAKED ON GRILL

(White, Sweet or Yams)

CHARCOAL—DIRECT OR INDIRECT METHOD
GAS—INDIRECT METHOD LOW HEAT

Prepare potatoes, wrapped or unwrapped, as directed in Potatoes Baked In 'Tater Grill (page 68) except arrange on cooking grill. Cover kettle and cook 45 to 60 minutes or until tender, turning potatoes once.

POTATOES BAKED IN 'TATER GRILL

(White, Sweet or Yams)

CHARCOAL—DIRECT METHOD
GAS—DIRECT METHOD LOW HEAT

Wash, dry and rub potato skins with oil, bacon fat or seasoned butter. Wrap each potato securely in double thick 8 to 10-inch square of heavy duty aluminum foil. Place in Corn 'N' Tater Grill. Set Tater Grill over cooking grill; cover kettle and bake 45 to 60 minutes, depending upon size of potato or until done. If a crisp skin is desired bake potatoes without wrapping in foil.

BAKED TOMATO HALVES

CHARCOAL—INDIRECT METHOD
GAS—INDIRECT METHOD LOW HEAT

Stem, wash and cut 4 large tomatoes in half cross-wise. Arrange halves, cut side up, in shallow baking pan. Melt ¼ cup butter or margarine. Brush tomato halves with 2 tablespoons melted butter or margarine. Add ⅓ cup fine dry bread crumbs and 2 teaspoons minced parsley to remaining butter or margarine; mix well. Stir in 2 tablespoons shredded Cheddar or grated Parmesan cheese. Spoon crumbs over tomatoes. Place on cooking grill; cover kettle and heat. Yield: 8 servings.

SWEET CORN COOKED IN FOIL

CHARCOAL—INDIRECT METHOD
GAS—INDIRECT METHOD LOW HEAT

Remove husks and silk from ears of corn. Allow 2 or 3 ears per person. Wash ears in cold water; drain. Spread ears with butter or margarine; season with salt and pepper. Wrap ears individually in a double thickness of heavy duty aluminum foil; fold top and ends securely. Place in Corn 'N' Tater Grill and set over cooking grill or place on cooking grill. Cover kettle and cook 25 to 30 minutes or until done, turning ears 2 or 3 times during cooking.

To test for doneness: Puncture a kernel with knife; corn is done if no milky juices escape.

CORN IN HUSKS

CHARCOAL—INDIRECT METHOD
GAS—INDIRECT METHOD LOW HEAT

Fold back husks carefully; remove silk. Tie husks at tip end and center; soak in cold water ½ hour. Remove ears from water, shake well; place in Corn 'N' Tater Grill and set over cooking grill or place directly on cooking grill. Cover kettle and cook 25 to 30 minutes or until done, turning ears 2 or 3 times during heating. Use gloves to remove husks.

ACORN SQUASH

CHARCOAL—INDIRECT METHOD
GAS—INDIRECT METHOD LOW HEAT

Select medium squash. Wash, dry and cut squash in half lengthwise; remove seeds. Prick inside of squash 8 to 10 times, about ¼-inch deep with tines of fork. Measure ½ tablespoon butter or margarine, 1 teaspoon water and 1 tablespoon brown sugar into cavity of each squash half. Sprinkle with salt. Place, cavity side up, on cooking grill; cover kettle and bake 50 to 60 minutes or until done. Do not turn during baking. Yield: ½ squash per person.

HERB OR ONION BAKED POTATO QUARTERS

CHARCOAL—INDIRECT METHOD
GAS—INDIRECT METHOD LOW HEAT

Wash, dry and quarter (lengthwise) unpared baking potatoes. Spread cut surfaces of each generously with Herb or Onion Butter (page 62). Reassemble potato. Wrap as directed for Potatoes Baked in 'Tater Grill (at left). Place on cooking grill, cover kettle and bake 40 to 60 minutes, depending on size of potato or until done.

STUFFED TOMATOES

CHARCOAL—INDIRECT METHOD
GAS—INDIRECT METHOD LOW HEAT

Cook 1 package (9 or 10 ounces) frozen peas or corn kernels as directed on page 67. Cut a thin slice from top of 4 medium tomatoes. Scoop out seeds and pulp. Place tomatoes, cavity up, in shallow baking pan. Season inside of tomatoes with salt and pepper. Add 3 tablespoons water to pan. Cover pan; place on cooking grill. Cover kettle and heat. Fill tomatoes with hot cooked vegetable; garnish with bits of green pepper or pimiento. Yield: 4 servings.

SCHAPER'S STUFFED MUSHROOMS

CHARCOAL—INDIRECT METHOD
GAS—INDIRECT METHOD LOW HEAT

1 pound medium mushrooms
¼ cup butter or margarine
⅓ cup fine dry bread crumbs
2 tablespoons grated Parmesan cheese
¼ teaspoon salt
Dash of pepper

Wash, dry and stem mushrooms. Melt butter or margarine over low heat; add crumbs and cheese and brown lightly, stirring constantly. Stir in salt and pepper. Stuff mushroom caps with crumb mixture; arrange on cookie sheet. Center on cooking grill. Cover kettle and cook 10 to 15 minutes or until mushrooms are tender. Yield: About 6 servings.

BAKED WHOLE EGGPLANT

CHARCOAL—INDIRECT METHOD
GAS—INDIRECT METHOD LOW HEAT

Prick medium eggplant on all sides with two-tined fork. Brush with melted butter or margarine and sprinkle with salt. Place on cooking grill over drip pan, cover kettle and bake 20 to 30 minutes or until tender, turning once. To serve, cut slices about ½-inch thick. Brush slices with melted butter or margarine and sprinkle with salt and pepper. Yield: About 6 servings.

POTATOES BOULANGERE

CHARCOAL—INDIRECT METHOD
GAS—INDIRECT METHOD LOW HEAT

8 medium potatoes, pared
2 medium onions, thinly sliced
1 tablespoon chopped parsley
1½ teaspoons salt
Dash of pepper
¼ cup butter or margarine
1 cup hot chicken or beef bouillon

Slice potatoes ¼-inch thick. Mix potatoes and onions. Season with parsley, salt and pepper. Spread about ½-inch deep in buttered shallow 2-quart baking dish. Dot with butter or margarine. Add bouillon. Place on cooking grill, cover kettle and bake 30 to 40 minutes or until potatoes are tender, brown and crusty on top and liquid disappears. Yield: About 8 servings.

RED CABBAGE WITH APPLES

CHARCOAL—INDIRECT METHOD
GAS—INDIRECT METHOD LOW HEAT

1 small head red cabbage, shredded
3 apples, pared, cored and thinly sliced
¼ cup salad oil, melted butter or margarine
½ cup apple juice
¼ cup red wine vinegar
¼ cup water
¼ cup sugar
1 teaspoon salt
¼ teaspoon thyme leaves, crushed
Dash of pepper

Combine ingredients; mix well. Turn into heavy 2-quart casserole or pot with heatproof handles. Cover casserole. Place on cooking grill; cover kettle and cook about 1 hour or until tender. Stir 2 or 3 times during cooking. Yield: About 4 servings.

*Eggplant page 69, Carrots page 67,
Zucchini page 67*

desserts

FRUIT KABOBS

CHARCOAL—INDIRECT METHOD
GAS—INDIRECT METHOD LOW HEAT

Arrange bite-size chunks of fruit such as fresh pineapple, unpeeled red plums, melon, bananas and
thick fresh peach slices in bowls on tray along with
Weber skewers. At serving time thread fruits on
skewers. Position and attach Weber Shish Kabob
Rack on cooking grill before heating grill. Arrange
filled skewers on rack and brush with Apricot Butter
or Basting Sauce (page 62). Cover kettle and cook
3 to 5 minutes or until hot and lightly browned, turning once or twice. Serve with additional sauce.
Sprinkle with coconut.

CHERRY DELIGHT

CHARCOAL—INDIRECT METHOD
GAS—INDIRECT METHOD LOW HEAT

1 can (1 pound) cherry pie filling
1 package (18½ ounces) yellow cake mix
½ cup butter or margarine, melted
1 can (3½ ounces) flaked coconut
½ cup chopped walnuts
1½ to 2 pints vanilla ice cream, optional

Spread cherry pie filling evenly over bottom of 8 x 8 x
2-inch square pan. Sprinkle yellow cake mix evenly
over fruit. Drizzle butter or margarine evenly over
cake mix. Sprinkle top with coconut and nuts. Center
on cooking grill; cover kettle and bake about 45 minutes or until done. Serve warm or chilled, plain or
topped with ice cream. Yield: 9 to 12 servings.

PEACHY-BERRY COBBLER

CHARCOAL—INDIRECT METHOD
GAS—INDIRECT METHOD LOW HEAT

3 tablespoons butter or margarine, melted
1 package (10 ounces) frozen sliced peaches,
   thawed
1 package (10 ounces) frozen red raspberries,
   thawed
1 teaspoon lemon juice
1 cup packaged biscuit mix
6 tablespoons sugar
1/3 cup milk or half and half
1/2 teaspoon cinnamon
Whipped cream or ice cream, optional

Pour first 4 ingredients into heavy metal 10-inch skillet or casserole with tight fitting cover and heat-proof handles and knob. Cover handles and knob with foil for extra protection. Place pan on cooking grill. Cover kettle and bring fruits to a boil while preparing topping. Combine biscuit mix, 3 tablespoons sugar and milk or half and half; stir just until dry ingredients are moistened. Drop spoonsful of dough onto boiling fruit mixture. Cover at once! Cover kettle and cook 10 to 15 minutes or until topping is cooked. Remove from heat. Combine and mix remaining 3 tablespoons sugar and cinnamon, sprinkle over crust; cover for 2 or 3 minutes. Serve warm, plain or topped with whipped cream or ice cream. Yield: 6 servings.

TRIPLE FUDGE BARS

CHARCOAL—INDIRECT METHOD
GAS—INDIRECT METHOD LOW HEAT

1 package (3¾ ounces) chocolate pudding and
   pie filling (not instant)
1 package (18½ ounces) chocolate cake mix
1 cup chocolate chips
1/2 cup chopped walnuts
Vanilla or chocolate ice cream, optional

Prepare pudding mix as directed on package label. Stir in dry chocolate cake mix. Pour into greased 9 x 13 x 2-inch pan. Sprinkle chocolate chips and walnuts over batter. Center pan on cooking grill; cover kettle and bake about 40 minutes or until done. Cool or serve warm. To serve, cut into squares; serve warm or cold, plain or with ice cream. Yield: 15 to 24 servings.

CHERRIES JUBILEE

1 can (1 pound) pitted dark sweet cherries
1/4 cup sugar
2 tablespoons cornstarch
Dash salt
1/4 teaspoon almond extract
1/3 cup brandy, kirsch or rum, optional
1 quart vanilla ice cream
1/3 cup toasted slivered almonds, optional

Drain cherries, reserving syrup. Add water to syrup, if necessary, to make 1 cup. Mix syrup, sugar, cornstarch and salt in blazer pan of chafing dish. Place over direct high flame; cook until sauce is clear and slightly thickened, stirring constantly. Fold in cherries, extract, and 2 tablespoons brandy, kirsch or rum; heat. Place pan over hot-water bath of chafing dish to keep hot for serving. If desired, just before serving pour remaining liquor over sauce and ignite. When flame dies spoon sauce over ice cream and, if desired, sprinkle with almonds. Yield: 6 servings.

GRILLED GRAPEFRUIT

CHARCOAL—INDIRECT METHOD
GAS—INDIRECT METHOD LOW HEAT

Cut grapefruit in half crosswise; remove seeds and cut membrane from fruit. Sprinkle each half with 1/2 teaspoon sugar. Center each grapefruit on an 8 to 10-inch square of aluminum foil; lift edges up around grapefruit. Drizzle 2 or 3 teaspoons creme de menthe or grenadine syrup over fruit. Center on cooking grill; cover kettle and heat 6 to 8 minutes.

BAKED BANANAS

CHARCOAL—INDIRECT METHOD
GAS—INDIRECT METHOD LOW HEAT

1/4 cup butter or margarine, melted
1/4 cup orange juice
1/4 cup firmly-packed brown sugar
1/4 cup rum, optional
1 tablespoon lemon juice
6 large firm bananas
Whipped cream or vanilla ice cream

Combine butter or margarine, orange juice, brown sugar, rum and lemon juice; mix well. Cut bananas in half crosswise and lengthwise. Arrange in shallow baking dish. Spoon sauce over bananas. Center on cooking grill; cover kettle and bake about 15 minutes or just until tender. Baste with sauce 2 or 3 times during baking. Serve hot topped with whipped cream or ice cream, if desired. Yield: 6 to 8 servings.

BRANDY ICE

¾ cup brandy
1 quart hand-packed vanilla ice cream, softened
   slightly
Nutmeg

Chill 8 parfait or dessert dishes or champagne glasses in freezer. Chill mixing bowl and spoons in freezer. *Quickly* mix brandy and ice cream just until blended. Mound into chilled serving dishes; return to freezer *at once* to firm. Before serving top with a dash of nutmeg. Yield: 6 to 8 servings.

STRAWBERRY GLAZED CHEESE CAKE

Crust:
2 cups fine vanilla wafer crumbs
⅓ cup sugar
¼ teaspoon salt
½ cup butter or margarine, melted

Filling:
2 packages (8 ounces each) cream cheese, at
   room temperature
¼ cup half and half
1 teaspoon grated lemon peel
½ teaspoon salt
4 eggs
1 tablespoon lemon juice
2 teaspoons vanilla
¾ cup sugar
¼ cup flour

Topping:
1 package (10 ounces) frozen sliced strawberries,
   thawed
¼ cup sugar
1 tablespoon cornstarch
1 pint fresh strawberries, washed, hulled and cut
   in half lengthwise

Prepare Crust: Combine crust ingredients; blend well. Press evenly over bottom and up 1¾-inches on sides of buttered 9-inch spring form pan. Bake in preheated 350° oven 5 minutes. Prepare Filling: Beat cream cheese, half and half, lemon peel and salt until smooth. Add eggs, one at a time, beating well after each addition. Blend in lemon juice and vanilla. Mix sugar and flour; blend into cheese mixture. Pour into crust. Bake in 350° oven 35 to 40 minutes or until firm. Chill in pan. Prepare Topping: Whiz thawed strawberries and juice in blender or put through sieve. Mix sugar and cornstarch in small saucepan. Stir in strawberry mixture. Bring to a boil over low heat, stirring constantly, until sauce is thickened; cool slightly. Top cheesecake with fresh strawberry halves, cut side down. Spoon glaze over strawberries; chill. Yield: 10 to 16 servings.

casseroles

STUFFED GREEN PEPPERS

CHARCOAL—INDIRECT METHOD
GAS—INDIRECT METHOD LOW HEAT

6 medium green peppers
1 tablespoon butter or margarine
½ pound ground chuck
¾ cup coarsely chopped onion
1 can (8 ounces) tomato sauce
1 can (6 ounces) tomato paste
½ package (7 ounces) elbow macaroni, cooked
   and drained
1 teaspoon salt
Dash of pepper
1 cup (4 ounces) shredded process American cheese

Cut a thin slice from stem end of peppers; remove seeds and membrane. Wash peppers and parboil in salted water about 5 minutes. Cool in cold water; drain. Melt butter or margarine in skillet. Add beef and onion; brown meat, stirring often. Add tomato sauce and paste, macaroni, salt and pepper; mix well. Fold in cheese. Fill peppers with mixture. Arrange in shallow baking dish or pan. Center on cooking grill. Cover kettle and cook 25 to 30 minutes or until piping hot. Yield: 6 servings.

BAKED ONIONS BY GEORGE

CHARCOAL—INDIRECT METHOD
GAS—INDIRECT METHOD LOW HEAT

2 large Bermuda onions, sliced and separated
   into rings
2 tablespoons butter
2 cups (8 ounces) shredded Swiss cheese
1 can (10½ ounces) cream of chicken soup
½ cup milk
1 teaspoon soy sauce
¼ teaspoon pepper
6 to 8 slices French bread, buttered on both sides

In large skillet cook onion rings in butter until tender. Arrange onions in greased 1½-quart baking dish; sprinkle cheese on top. Blend soup, milk, soy sauce and pepper. Pour over cheese and onions and mix lightly. Arrange buttered bread slices over top. Center baking dish on cooking grill; cover kettle and cook 30 minutes. Yield: 4 to 6 servings.

CRANBERRY GLAZED
SWEET POTATOES

CHARCOAL—INDIRECT METHOD
GAS—INDIRECT METHOD LOW HEAT

2 cans (1 pound each) sweet potatoes, drained
1 cup whole cranberry sauce
¼ cup light corn syrup
2 tablespoons butter or margarine, melted
2 tablespoons sugar
1½ tablespoons grated orange peel
¾ teaspoon salt

Arrange sweet potatoes in shallow baking dish. Combine remaining ingredients in saucepan: bring to simmering stage and simmer 2 or 3 minutes. Spoon sauce over sweet potatoes; cover with aluminum foil. Center on cooking grill; cover kettle and heat about 30 minutes or until piping hot. Yield: 4 to 6 servings.

SCALLOPED POTATOES AND HAM

CHARCOAL—INDIRECT METHOD
GAS—INDIRECT METHOD LOW HEAT

4 cups thinly sliced (⅛-inch) pared potatoes
2 tablespoons chopped onion
1 to 1½ cups cubed (¾-inch) fully-cooked ham
1½ teaspoons salt
Dash of pepper
2 cups Medium White Sauce (page 61)

Grease shallow 2 to 3-quart baking dish or pan.
Spread ⅓ of potato slices over bottom of pan;
sprinkle with ⅓ of the onion, ham, salt and pepper
and pour ⅓ of white sauce over. Repeat 2 times.
Center uncovered pan on cooking grill; cover kettle
and bake about 1 hour 15 minutes or until potatoes
are fork tender. Yield: 4 to 6 servings.

BAKED BEANS

CHARCOAL—INDIRECT METHOD
GAS—INDIRECT METHOD LOW HEAT

1 can (31 ounces) pork and beans with tomato sauce
¼ cup firmly-packed brown sugar
1 small onion, finely chopped
¼ cup catsup
2 tablespoons molasses
1 teaspoon prepared mustard
½ teaspoon salt
Dash of pepper
3 slices bacon, cut in quarters

Combine and mix first 8 ingredients; pour into casserole. Cover beans with bacon pieces. Center casserole on cooking grill; cover kettle and heat about
45 minutes or until piping hot. Yield: 4 to 6 servings.

CHICKEN RICE

CHARCOAL—INDIRECT METHOD
GAS—INDIRECT METHOD LOW HEAT

1 can (10½ ounces) cream of mushroom soup
1 can (10½ ounces) cream of chicken soup
2⅔ cups water
1 package (1⅜ ounces) dry onion soup mix
1 cup uncooked rice
3-pound broiler-fryer, cut into serving pieces
2 tablespoons butter or margarine, melted
1 teaspoon salt
¼ teaspoon pepper

Combine and mix first 5 ingredients; pour into 9 x 13
x 2-inch baking pan or dish. Add chicken pieces;
brush with butter or margarine. Sprinkle salt and
pepper evenly over top. Cover pan tightly with aluminum foil. Center pan on cooking grill; cover kettle
and bake 1 hour. Remove foil and bake 20 to 25
minutes longer, or until chicken is fork tender. Yield:
About 4 servings.

SWEET POTATO CASSEROLE WITH PECAN TOPPING

CHARCOAL—INDIRECT METHOD
GAS—INDIRECT METHOD LOW HEAT

4 cups mashed cooked sweet potatoes (2 to
    2½ pounds)
1 egg, beaten
6 tablespoons firmly-packed brown sugar
6 tablespoons butter or margarine, melted
2 tablespoons orange juice
1 teaspoon salt
⅔ cup coarsely chopped pecans

Combine potatoes, egg, 3 tablespoons each of
brown sugar and butter or margarine, orange juice
and salt; beat until light and fluffy. Fold in ⅓ cup
pecans. Turn into buttered shallow 1½-quart casserole. Sprinkle remaining ⅓ cup nuts and 3 tablespoons brown sugar over top. Drizzle remaining 3
tablespoons butter or margarine over top. Center on
cooking grill; cover kettle and heat 30 minutes.
Yield: About 6 servings.

POTATO-CHEESE CASSEROLE

CHARCOAL—INDIRECT METHOD
GAS—INDIRECT METHOD LOW HEAT

1 can (10½ ounces) cream of chicken soup
¾ cup milk
1 cup (4 ounces) shredded process American or
    Cheddar cheese
4 medium potatoes, pared and thinly sliced
    (about ⅛-inch)
2 tablespoons finely chopped onion
1½ teaspoons salt
Dash of pepper
1 tablespoon butter or margarine
½ teaspoon minced parsley

Combine chicken soup, milk, ½ cup cheese, potatoes, onion, salt and pepper; mix. Pour into shallow
2-quart casserole; dot with butter or margarine.
Sprinkle remaining cheese and parsley over top.
Center casserole on cooking grill; cover kettle and
bake 1 hour 15 to 20 minutes or until potatoes are
fork tender. Yield: 4 to 6 servings.

beverages

COFFEE FOR A CROWD

CHARCOAL—INDIRECT METHOD
GAS—INDIRECT METHOD LOW HEAT

Count on 2 (6-ounce) servings of coffee for each guest. For 50 servings follow directions given below.

Use 1 pound regular grind coffee and 7 quarts water. Prepare as directed on package label or as follows.

Soak a clean heavy cloth sack or large square of 4 thicknesses of cheesecloth in cold water. Add coffee to bag or center in cheesecloth square. Pick up edges of cheesecloth and tie cloth or bag with clean heavy string, leaving enough string to allow bag to be attached to handle of pot, and enough space for coffee to expand. In large sauce pot heat measured amount of water to a full rolling boil. Reduce heat or push to coolest part of grill to keep water just below a boil. Lower coffee into water tying string ends to pot handle. Brew 6 to 8 minutes or until desired strength. Remove coffee sack.

CAMPFIRE COFFEE

CHARCOAL—INDIRECT METHOD
GAS—INDIRECT METHOD LOW HEAT

Bring 2 quarts of water to a boil. Stir 1 egg and 3 tablespoons cold water into 1 cup regular grind coffee. Turn into a 3 or 4-quart coffee pot. Pour boiling water over coffee. Bring to a boil. Cover; place to coolest side of grill; let stand 10 to 12 minutes. Just before serving pour ¼ cup cold water into coffee to clarify. Yield: About 10 to 12 servings.

ICED TEA

4 tablespoons tea leaves
3 cups boiling water
3 cups cold water
Crushed ice

Place tea in scalded teapot. Pour in boiling water and steep 4 to 5 minutes. Strain; stir in cold water. Pour over crushed ice. Serve with lemon wedges and mint sprigs. Yield: 8 servings.

LEMONADE COOLERS

Combine 1½ cups sugar, 1 cup water and 2 tablespoons grated lemon peel in saucepan. Bring to a boil; boil 5 minutes. Strain and chill. Add 1 cup lemon juice. At serving time fill 8-ounce glasses with crushed ice. To each glass add 2 tablespoons lemon mixture, a lemon slice and 1 or 2 maraschino cherries. Add water to fill; stir. Garnish with mint sprigs. Yield: About 16 servings.

FRUIT PUNCH FOR 25

Thaw 1 can (6 ounces) *each* of frozen limeade, orange juice and pineapple juice concentrate. Stir 1 tablespoon instant tea into 1 cup hot water; add to fruit juices; chill thoroughly. At serving time pour juices into chilled bowl; stir in 4 cups ice water, 1½ cups apricot nectar, ⅓ cup grenadine syrup, if desired, and 4 cups crushed ice. One pint of light rum may be added, if desired. Serve in punch or wine glasses. Garnish with mint sprigs. Yield: About 25 servings.

ALOHA PARTY PUNCH

Thaw 1 can (6 ounces) *each* of frozen orange juice, pineapple juice, and limeade concentrate; pour into chilled punch bowl. Stir in 4 cups ice water. Add 1 bottle (16 ounces) chilled carbonated water; stir gently. Scoop 1 quart vanilla ice cream into punch. Garnish with thin lime and orange slices and strawberry halves. Yield: About 3 quarts.

STRAWBERRY ICE CREAM PUNCH

Thaw 1 can (6 ounces) frozen pineapple juice concentrate and 1 package (10 ounces) frozen strawberries; pour into bowl. Stir in 1 pint slightly softened strawberry ice cream. Pour into chilled punch bowl. Add 4 bottles (7 ounces each) chilled lemon-lime carbonated beverage; stir gently. Spoon 1 pint strawberry ice cream over top. Serve in chilled punch cups or champagne glasses. Yield: About 2 quarts, or 25 to 30 servings.

wine chart

TYPE	WINE	DESCRIPTION	SERVE WITH	TEMPERATURE
Appetizer	Sherry	Dry or Cocktail	With or without foods	Room temperature, slightly chilled or over ice
	Vermouth (herb-flavored)	Dry or Sweet	With or without foods	Slightly chilled or over ice
White Dinner	Rhine, Riesling, Chablis, White Chianti	Light-bodied	Broiled or poached fish or seafood, omelets, soufflés, cheese fondues	Chilled 1 to 3 hours
	White Burgundy, Sauterne, Pinot Blanc	Full-bodied	Poultry, pork, veal dishes, fish or seafood with rich sauces	Same as above
Red Dinner	Beaujolais, Zinfandel, Gamay	Light-bodied	Duck, lamb, ham, pheasant	Cool room temperature
	Claret, Pinot Noir, Red Burgundy, Red Chianti, Cabernet Sauvignon	Medium to Full-bodied	Beef, spaghetti, barbecued foods, strong cheese, venison, wild duck	Same as above
Others	Rosé		Combination of hot or cold foods, ham	Chilled 1 to 3 hours
	Sake (Rice Wine)		Oriental foods	Slightly warmed or room temperature
Sparkling	Champagne	Dry to Sweet; Brut to Sec	Accompanies whole meal— sweet for dessert; dry for appetizer	Chilled 4 to 6 hours
	Crackling Rosé and Pink Champagne		Combination of foods, chicken, fish, seafood	Same as above
	Cold Duck (Burgundy and Champagne)		Combination of foods	Same as above
	Sparkling Burgundy		Meats and game	Same as above
Dessert	Sherry	Sweet or Cream	Desserts or refreshment	Room temperature or slightly chilled
	Haut Sauterne (Sweet)		Cakes, pound or unfrosted, dessert mouses, soufflés	Chilled 1 to 3 hours
	Port	Ruby, White or Tawny	Cheese, fruit (except acid ones), nuts	Room temperature
	Muscatel		Fruit, nuts	Same as above

index